WHY WE LEFT ISLAM

WHY WE LEFT ISLAM

FORMER MUSLIMS SPEAK OUT

COMPILED AND EDITED

BY

SUSAN CRIMP

AND

JOEL RICHARDSON

WND BOOKS

WHY WE LEFT ISLAM: Former Muslims Speak Out
A WND Book
Published by WND Books, Inc.
Los Angeles, CA

WND Books are distributed to the trade by:

Midpoint Trade Books
27 West 20th Street, Suite 1102
New York, NY 10011

WND Books books are available at special discounts for bulk purchases. WND Books, Inc. also publishes books in electronic formats. For more information call (310) 961-4170 or visit www.wndbooks.com.

First Edition

ISBN 10-Digit 0979267102
ISBN 13-Digit 9780979267109
Library of Congress Control Number: 2007943650

Printed in the United States of America

10 9 8 7 6 5 4 3 2 1

We dedicate this book to the thousands of innocent individuals murdered in the name of Islam—the men and women lost on September 11, 2001, in the Bali and Madrid and London bombings, and in the attacks in India and Pakistan—as well as the countless men and women killed in Iraq and in other attacks throughout the world. (Since September 11, 2001, Islamic terrorists have carried out more than ten thousand deadly terror attacks.)

We dedicate this book also to the innocent schoolchildren barbarically slaughtered in Russia and to Sister Leonella, an elderly Catholic nun who spent a lifetime loving Muslims only to be repaid with a bullet in her back. This book is also written so that the victims of Islamic regimes who endure death by stoning, amputation of limbs for theft, and who live in fear of death because they leave Islam, may not be forgotten. Our intention is that, in reading the collection of stories, the world will clearly hear their cries for justice and their cries for freedom.

"If any religion allows the persecution of the people of different faiths, if any religion keeps women in slavery, if any religion keeps people in ignorance, then I can't accept that religion."[1]

—Tasmila Nasrin: Physician and Author

"There is no truth on earth but monotheism and following tenets of Islam and there is no way for salvation of mankind but the rule of Islam over mankind."[2]

—Iranian President Mahmoud Ahmadinejad

"Even if we were to agree that the vast majority of Muslims are 'moderates' and that, say, only a mere 20 percent of Muslims are 'literalists,' that means that some 250 million Muslims in the world today are dedicated enemies of the infidel West."[3]

—Raymond Ibraham

"...on September 11, 2001, I saw the real face of Islam. I saw the happiness on the faces of our people because so many infidels were slaughtered so easily. I was shocked at the gloating of our people for killing innocent kafirs [unbelievers]. I saw many people who started thanking Allah for this massacre. Our Islamic people said that Allah gave us our wish, and that this was the beginning of the destruction of kafir countries. To me, this was sheer inhumanity. Then, the imam implored Allah to help the Taliban against the U.S. military. I was angry. It was then that I stopped praying."[4]

—Khaled Waleed, Saudi Arabia

CONTENTS

PREFACE

BEFORE BEGINNING, it is necessary to briefly review some basic facts and terms about Islam and its authority structure. The first and most well-known of Islam's sacred books is of course the Qur'an. The Qur'an may somewhat be viewed as the Bible of Islam in that it is the primary holy book of Islam. The Qur'an was conveyed entirely by Mohammad, the founder and "Prophet" of Islam. The word "Qur'an" means "recitation" or "reading" in Arabic. The book consists of 114 chapters called *surahs*.

The Qur'an, however, is not the only source of sacred or even inspired traditions in Islam. For while it is the only Islamic text said to be the literal words of Allah, equally important to all Muslims is the *Sunna*. Much of the Sunna is found in several collections of traditions known as *Hadith*. Remember that word, as it will be used much throughout this book. "The Sunna" in Arabic literally means, "a clear or well trodden path." The word refers to whatever Mohammad said, did, condoned, or condemned. It is the record of Mohammad's sayings, customs, teachings, or the example that he left for all Muslims to follow. Muslims view Mohammad as the perfect example for all human beings. This doctrine is spelled out quite clearly in the Qur'an:

> If you love Allah, then follow me (Mohammad) *Qur'an 3:31* (Shakir)

Whatever Mohammad did or said, therefore, becomes the basis from which to model all life and belief. The Sunna is as important as the Qur'an because it interprets the Qur'an. Without the Sunna, the Qur'an cannot be properly understood. In fact, many aspects and practices of the Islamic religion are not mentioned in the Qur'an but are found only in the Sunna. Therefore, the Qur'an and the Sunna together form the basis for the beliefs and practices of Muslims everywhere. In this sense, both the Qur'an and the Sunna are believed to be inspired and authoritative. When confronted with some of the more violent or base teachings or practices of Islam, most Muslim apologists will simply ask the question, "Where is that in the Qur'an?" This is a purposeful attempt to mislead the questioner. For, as stated above, whether a teaching is found in the Qur'an or only in the Sunna, it is an essential aspect of Islam.

ACKNOWLEDGMENTS

THIS BOOK would not be possible without the cooperation of some extremely brave men and women who agreed to share their stories, for which they could face death. As a result, some have chosen to remain anonymous or use pseudonyms to protect themselves. Others included here have even entered the Witness Protection Program. Despite the price that this act of witness demands, they have been brave enough to come forward and tell their stories. While some cannot be thanked by name, their cooperation and courage are beyond commendable.

Special thanks also go to other tireless heroes. Parvin Darabi has worked tirelessly to bring global attention to the problems facing women in the Islamic world. Robert Spencer of Jihad Watch and Jochen Katz of Answering-Islam.org have labored for years correcting fundamentalist propaganda and providing responses and solid answers for searching hearts and minds.

Gratitude is also extended to Maxine Fiel for her contribution, as well as to Mara Einstein for the expertise she offered to help bring this project to fruition. In addition, we thank all of those who have been brave enough to break out of their own personal prisons by standing up to tyranny. Finally, we extend our deepest and most heartfelt gratitude to the memory of those who have made the ultimate sacrifice.

INTRODUCTION

D UE TO THE SUBJECT MATTER of this book, we can already hear the potential cries and chants of "Death to the authors. Death to the editors. Death to the publishers." Indeed, it is sadly true that the simple expression of one of the West's greatest freedoms, namely the freedom of speech, could result in danger to all involved in this project. However, in this time of global Islamofascist terrorism and crippling political correctness, there is too much at stake to capitulate to fear.

While we acknowledge that there are millions of Muslims who want to live quiet and peaceful lives, it is not these Muslims that this book is about. This book is about the other side of Islam—the side of Islam that refuses to live in peace with the non-Islamic world. Even for those individuals who would rather not rock the boat, there must come a point when enough is enough. When the Sudanese government jails a teacher because her pupils name a teddy bear Mohammad[1], or when mobs brutally pillage and murder over a depiction of Islam's Prophet in a cartoon[2], or when a sixty-five-year-old Catholic nun dies because of a reference Pope Benedict XVI made about Mohammad[3], surely it is time to pause and examine the state of our world and, specifically, the state and purpose of Islam itself.

In recent years we have seen calls for world leaders to convert to Islam.[4] We have seen Pakistan's Benazair Bhutto assassinated.[5] Islam has inserted itself into the global public square and so has opened itself to examination. What you will read here expresses the concerns of many former Muslims about the imposition of Islam on their lives. Their desire to speak candidly is born from their concern about what they have seen from within.

This collection of stories perhaps better than any other exemplifies the spirit of what makes the West great—the freedom to speak, to query, to challenge, and even to reject. We in the West value religious freedom and generally respect other world religions. Because Islam is categorized, viewed, and understood merely as a religion, many hesitate to participate in any discourse critical of it.

The problem with this thinking is that Islam is not merely a religion; it is also a full-fledged global political movement that seeks to impose its ways onto every human being on the planet. As such, Islam is far more than a religion; it is also a detailed legal system and, as many Muslim scholars have expressed, a complete way of life. So, while it is perfectly acceptable in any public forum to criticize capitalism or monarchism, it is a serious violation of modern political correctness to criticize Islam. However, as an ideology, it may fairly be compared to any other ideology. But, as you will discover, Islam prohibits the type of examination or criticism that this book entails and even offers fatal punishments for any criticism. Whatever side of the political spectrum you lean toward, this prohibition should deeply concern us all.

This book you now hold arrives at an important juncture in world history, for while millions of Muslims throughout the world increasingly embrace more radical forms of Islam, millions more choose to abandon their faith altogether. Yet while we may read about the opinions, thoughts, and activities of radical Muslims throughout the world, the other side of the story is rarely heard. These former Muslims walk away for various reasons: some to join other religions, some to leave behind religion altogether. However, for the most part, these so-called "apostates" depart because they feel that Islam allows little space for individual freedom; nor does it suitably value human life. Many concluded that Islam does not promote tolerance or individual rights but instead offers suppression and intolerance.

Now some of these individuals have chosen to bear witness. The courage of that choice is evidenced by the many who leave Islam and die for doing so. This is in accordance with the commandment of the Prophet Mohammad, who stated that "Whoever changes his religion, kill him."[6] Despite these dangers, these brave individuals have spoken out.

The following letters have been collected over the past five years. Some of the individuals are former radical Muslims, while

others were peaceful and moderate Muslims. This mosaic of stories is but a small representation of the growing multitude that
believes that despite the great dangers inherent in speaking out,
the danger of remaining silent is far greater. The former risks a
life; the latter jeopardizes the future for everyone.

Many Muslims and non-Muslims alike have claimed that the
terrorists have hijacked this "religion of peace," and that Islam
does not condone violence. Yet many of these witnesses challenge
this notion. Who then shall we believe? Through this collage of
stories, we are better able to assess this argument ourselves—
deciding between what has come to be a popular belief, and the
consistent testimony of these many living witnesses. In this age
when radical Islam dominates the headlines, it is important that
all of us in the West wrestle with these questions and make ourselves aware of the truth concerning Islam.

One strand of thought that consistently runs through these testimonies is that the only real way to understand the true spirit of
Islam is to look at the complete picture formed by the Qur'an, the
traditions of Mohammad, and the history of Islam itself. While
many in the West continue to wrestle with whether radical Islam's
hatred of the West is inspired by American foreign policy or due to
its support for the state of Israel, many radical Muslims see the
present *jihad* against the West as a continuation of a battle lost on
none other than September 11, *1683*.

On that fateful day, Western forces in Vienna defeated the
forces of the Islamic Ottoman Empire.[7] Many radical Muslims believe the latest wave of *jihad* against the West is rooted in a far older battle—the foundation of which was laid long before the forma-
tion of America and the state of Israel and whose ultimate goal is
Islamic global domination. The West must recognize what is at
stake in the present global clash of ideologies. Whether it is al-
Qaeda, Hizb-ut-Tahrir, Hizbullah, or any of the various Islamist
groups or movements daily multiplying throughout the world, the
goals of radical Islamofacism remain the same.

The first goal is the destruction and subjugation of Israel,
America, and the West. This action is carried out through acts of
terror, but the subsequent ramifications become both economic

and political. The second goal is the establishment of a worldwide Islamic state known as a caliphate that will enforce Islamic law throughout the world. Even though nations with Judeo-Christian roots universally surpass Islamic nations in terms of freedom and human rights, we are expected to believe Islam provides mankind with a better source of justice and human rights. However, even within the best examples of Islamist nations in the world today, we do not see the promotion of human rights and justice, but instead only oppression and darkness. Consequently, what is at stake is freedom, human rights, and the very dignity of the human race.

If this seems too alarmist, then consider the words of Sheikh Mubarak Gilani, who has said, "Say, 'Victory is in the air!' The *kafir's* [non-Muslim's] blood will not be spared."[8] Why should the *sheikh's* words mean anything to us? Who is Sheikh Mubarak Gilani? Gilani is the founder of Jamaat al-Fuqra (Community of the Poor), a terror organization that has been "linked to seventeen fire bombings and ten assassinations in the United States alone."[9]

In January 2002, when *Wall Street Journal* reporter Daniel Pearl was kidnapped and then beheaded, Sheikh Gilani became infamous as the cleric with which Pearl was hoping to meet when Pearl met his tragic fate.[10] The U.S. State Department claims Gilani has said that the goal of his organization is to "purify Islam through violence."[11] The horrifying reality is that Sheikh Gilani's network of terror was not started in Afghanistan, but in the 1980s in Brooklyn, New York.[12] Gilani immediately began looking for members. In a recruitment video, the *sheikh* clearly established his mission:

> We have reached out and prepared [recruits] to defend themselves in a highly specialized training of guerrilla warfare... We are at present establishing training camps... We are not fighting so that the enemy recognizes us and offers something. We are fighting to destroy the enemy. We are dealing with evil at its roots and its roots are America.[13]

What should alarm all Americans and people throughout the free world is that Gilani's training camps are found throughout the United States. In fact, according to extensive research conducted by Paul L. Williams, author of *The Day of Islam*, there is one in Hancock, New York, located on seventy acres, called Islamberg.

There are also other facilities, or *hamaats* as they are called, across the United States: in Deposit, New York; Hyattsville, Maryland; Red House, Virginia; Falls Church, Virginia; Macon, Georgia; York, South Carolina; Dover, Tennessee; Buena Vista, Colorado; Talihina, Oklahoma; Tulane County California; Commerce, California; and Onalaska, Washington.[14]

Each of these compounds was set up for young Muslims — many of whom are converts — enabling them to begin a "new life." However, before becoming a citizen at any of these facilities the recruits must sign an oath that says: "I shall always hear and obey, and whenever given the command, I shall readily fight for Allah's sake."[15] These training camps have sent scores of American Muslims to Pakistan each year for guerrilla training. [16] Some local residents who live near the Hancock compound have voiced their concerns to no avail. Neighbors of the compound report the frequent sound of gunfire and small explosions, and armed guards wearing traditional Middle Eastern attire keep any visitors from entering the camp.[17] Again, this is in upstate New York. It is compounds like these that many rightly fear may be breeding grounds for fundamentalist hatred as that voiced by Sheikh Gilani.

If Islamism continues to grow in numbers and its acidic ideology is left unchecked, then we are indeed without hope. Bernard Lewis, one of the greatest modern scholars of the Middle East, warned that democracy could never develop side by side with Islam: "Their creed and political program are not compatible with liberal democracy."[18] If the values of liberal democracy are to survive, then the West must first begin to understand the seriousness of the present war of ideas. These testimonies are offered so that those of us on the outside may begin to truly understand Islam from the inside.

These writers speak candidly, often with sadness. Many who have known Islam from birth believe the terrorists' interpretation of Islam is correct — that in fact the terrorists who carry out the atrocities we are witnessing on a global scale are following the true model of their Prophet Mohammad. These letters are a conversation, testimonials that reflect the dialogue of what is happening, both within and outside of Islam. These people have agreed to come forward and to speak, thinking that if truth has ever mattered, it matters most *now*. They firmly believe *this* is the time to expose and acknowledge the root of the problem.

Herein is a group of ex-Muslims, many who feel that they have seen the face of evil and have risen to expose it. They do so in the conviction that no matter how painful the truth, only the truth can set one free. They speak also to other Muslims; urging those from within their communities to end the excuses, justifications, and rationalizations; to stop dividing mankind into "us" and "them" — the Muslims versus the *kafirs*. They speak of freedom to choose one's faith, and of killings perpetrated in the name of Allah. Furthermore, they urge non-Muslims to speak beyond the politically correct rhetoric, and to offer a critique of Islam that is honest and productive. They want above all to save lives, to end oppression, and to stop the onward march of Islamic fundamentalism.

CHAPTER ONE

MY SISTER

"She finally decided to protest the oppression of women by setting herself on fire in a crowded square in northern Tehran on February 21, 1994. Her last cries were: 'Death to tyranny! Long live liberty! Long live Iran!'"

ON SEPTEMBER 11, 2001, the world saw the seventh century mentality of fundamentalist Islam gain possession of twenty-first century technology. The results were catastrophic. The violent nature of Islam arrived on American soil—unforgettably and irrevocably. Many Americans, along with other Westerners, hadn't thought much about Islam before then. September 11 changed all that, bringing Islam home to the twenty-first century Western world. Suddenly, Iran and Iraq didn't seem so far away after all, and Westerners, especially we Americans, wanted to learn more about this faceless enemy who'd declared war on us in the most barbaric way imaginable. We found ourselves confronted with a deadly force that we'd thought lay half a world away and fourteen centuries in the past. Those terrorist bombings we'd heard of only on television had moved from a faraway Middle East to our own backyard. On September 11, what Islam represents became one of the most important questions facing the Western world, and our first experience with it left a bitter taste in many American mouths.

Parvin Darabi doesn't just *talk* about the barbarity of radical Islam that Americans experienced that day—she'd *lived* it long before the Twin Towers fell. In this poignant and painful letter, she writes of her sister, Homa, who struggled mightily against the heavy hand of the Islamic government in Iran. Living as a woman carries a heavy price in Iran. Homa was willing to pay it. Now Parvin carries on, and she urges us all to ignore the peaceful rhetoric of Islam and focus instead on the violent reality of Islamic rule. What Homa Darabi experienced in Iran could one day come to the West if Islamofascist terrorism is not defeated. Homa's story is a specific example of how an Islamic government works—and why it would never work in the West.

My Sister

My sister, Dr. Homa Darabi, was born in Tehran, Iran, in January 1940, two months premature, to Eshrat Dastyar, a child bride who at age thirteen had married Esmaeil Darabi. Homa was my older sister, my protector, and my role model. Homa had a life full of hope and promise that a tyrannical and fundamentalist Islamic system destroyed.

Indeed, my sister could never have imagined what lay ahead for her as she completed her elementary and high school education in Tehran. She then immediately entered the University of Tehran's School of Medicine after passing the university's entrance exam in 1959. It was a marvelous accomplishment and one that made our family proud. Homa was in the first 150 out of thousands of students who took the examination and became one of the three hundred who were accepted (the medical school's capacity).

A feisty and spirited young woman, my sister became quite active in politics and hoped to bring human rights and equal status for women in Iran. Her dream was most evident during her days in high school and in her freshman year at the university. Yet her quest would not be easy. In 1960, as a result of her efforts, she was arrested and imprisoned for a while, during the students' protests against the oppressive regime of the Shah. The regime was especially hostile towards students and youth who were beginning to demand more freedom of expression, assembly, and speech.

In 1963, my sister married her classmate, Manoochehr Keyhani, presently a prominent hematologist. Together they brought into this world two intelligent daughters.

Following the completion of her studies at the University of Tehran, Dr. Darabi practiced for two years in Bahmanier, a village in northern Iran, while her husband completed his military

2

obligation as a physician in the Iranian health corps. In 1968, she and her husband passed the Education Council Foreign Medical Graduates (ECFMG) examination and came to the United States to further their education. She took her residency in pediatrics and later specialized in psychiatry and then in child psychiatry and was licensed to practice medicine in the states of New Jersey, New York, and California. She became a naturalized citizen of the United States in the mid-1970s.

Due to pressures from her husband and family and her desire to give back to her native country, she returned to Iran in 1976 and was immediately accepted as a professor at the University of Tehran School of Medicine.

She was the first Iranian ever to pass the board in child psychiatry in the U.S. and was the driving force behind the establishment of the Psychiatric Clinic of Shahid Sahami in Tehran.

Although she was a strong supporter of the revolution, my sister opposed the establishment of an Islamic republic. Furthermore, when her party leader took advantage of the new Islamic guidelines and took a second wife, Homa was devastated and totally broke away from all politics. My sister then devoted her time to her profession as a medical doctor.

In 1990, due to her non-compliance with wearing the *hijab* (covering up of women), she was fired from her position as a professor at the School of Medicine.

Later, my sister was harassed in her practice for the same reason until finally, when life was made too difficult for her, she closed down her practice and became a full-time housewife for the first time in her life.

During her professional life my sister was under pressure from some parents of her younger patients to give the label of "mentally incapacitated" to many perfectly intelligent young girls so that they could be saved from the tortures of the zealots (150 strokes of a whip for things such as wearing makeup or lipstick). Having to label these young women truly broke my sister's heart.

When a sixteen-year-old girl was shot to death in northern Tehran for wearing lipstick, my sister could no longer handle the guilt she felt about her former involvement in the Iranian

Revolution. My sister felt Iran had been hijacked by the religious factions, and the way women were treated in Iran was unforgivable.... She wanted the world to know what was happening. She finally decided to protest the oppression of women by setting herself on fire in a crowded square in northern Tehran on February 21, 1994. Her last cries were:

> Death to tyranny!
>
> Long live liberty!
>
> Long live Iran![1]

My sister came to this world prematurely, and died prematurely.

Today, millions of people, especially women, are still echoing my sister's last cry, yet, sadly, few are listening. It is because of this that I wrote my book *Rage Against the Veil*. It is presented in the hope that the West and particularly America begins to understand the enormity of the problem. How just like in Iran, Islam is now universally being presented as a peaceful religion when ultimately it is a fascist form of government which is most evident in my former nation. This was a problem that my own sister was prepared to sacrifice her precious life for and I am writing about it now in order to help preserve everything we in the West hold dear. My story is an attempt to try through education and awareness to prevent what happened in Iran from happening throughout the entire world.

My sister Homa believed it was worth dying to bring attention to the problems of fundamentalist Islamic regimes. She died in order to preserve liberty and the country of Iran, which she loved. Today, Homa would be horrified to know how even more extreme and fundamental Iran has become and devastated to learn about the examples of Islamic tyranny and terrorism which exist in other parts of the world today. Yet, while it may be hard for many to understand what women inside of these radical regimes experience and why, the words of the Prophet Mohammad himself allow us to gain insight into why this is permitted. Indeed, it is from the mouth of the man most emulated within Islam itself, the Prophet Mohammad, that we learn exactly how women are regarded in

Islamic culture and how many actions within the Islamic world toward women reflect Mohammad's sentiments.

> I was standing at the edge of the fire (hell) and the majority of the people going in were women. *Prophet Mohammad*[2]

Ever since I began my activities in exposing Islam and its oppression of women, I have been attacked by Muslim men and a few Muslim women about what they say is my misconception and misinterpretation of Islamic laws regarding women. I have been told that Islam is a religion of peace and equality; that Islam has a high regard for women, and that Islamic laws have given women power. However, I have seen little evidence of this and certainly virtually nothing written in the Qur'an.

In fact, in the back of one edition of the Qur'an translated into English by M.H. Shakir, it is stated that:

> The Qur'an is a complete and original compilation of the Final Revelation from God to mankind through the last prophet, the Prophet of Islam, Mohammad. The Qur'an has essentially three qualities that make it universal. First, in its original Arabic form, it is a masterpiece of immense literary value—fusing the style of presentation with the substance being presented in a blend of unique proportions. Second, though its message is a continuation of that contained in the earlier Revelations made to Abraham, David, Moses and Jesus, yet this message has a sense of fulfillment and originality that attracts toward it Jews, Christians and Muslims alike. Finally, it has a wealth of information—which provides the code of life for mankind generally and Muslims in particular. Indeed, the Qur'an's miracle lies in its ability to offer at least something to non-believers and everything to believers.[3]

I would like to analyze some of these "immense literary values" presented in the Qur'an regarding women. I would like to find where it is that Islam has placed women on a pedestal for men to worship. And how it is that if we women were given so many rights by this book, then why we are not able to assert ourselves as human beings, but instead remain subjected to tyranny in Islamic countries?

Let's begin with the notion that Islam is a religion of peace. "Islam" in Arabic means "submission." Therefore, if we as people

5

would submit to the rules and laws of Islam, we will have peace. What exactly does this mean? Well, by my calculation based on my own experiences within Islamic regimes, it seems that as long as we accept that women were created inferior to men; that limbs can be cut off for theft; that people should face stoning for such crimes as adultery; and that men have the right to divorce, sole custody of their children, and multiple wives—then we can live in peace. Additionally, we can have peace as long as one prays five times a day, goes to mosque every Friday, and women sit in the back behind the men. Furthermore, in this peaceful scenario we must also accept that any inheritance allows a man's share to be twice that of women. We must also bear in mind, however, that we must never, ever criticize Mohammad or the fine religion of Islam, otherwise we cannot have peace. Also, if a person like author Taslima Nasrin, or Ayaan Hirsi Ali, or myself, criticizes Islam we must endure the wrath of the good Muslims and endure multiple threats to our lives. I ask you: Is this peace?

It is indeed difficult to find any way to attribute the word "peace" to Islam, especially when we consider that a filmmaker such as Theo Van Gogh makes a documentary about the life of a Muslim woman to show the atrocities she must endure and then he is brutally murdered. This is peace? Furthermore, when a Danish paper published cartoons of the Prophet, these so-called "peaceful Muslims" carried signs of violence, and created bloodshed all over Europe and throughout the Islamic world.

Is this a peaceful religion which allows killing over the publication of some cartoons? I suggest that it is very difficult to understand any of this equating in any way to peace. Yet maybe the Qur'an itself sets forth the tone for such behavior? Here are some of the revelations in the Qur'an regarding the religion of peace, which may explain why millions of followers of this book behave the way they do. In the Qur'an it is written:

> And kill them wherever you find them and drive them out whence they drive you out. *Qur'an 2:191*

> Surely they who disbelieve in the communication of Allah— they shall have a severe chastisement. *Qur'an 3:4*

Say to those who disbelieve: you shall be vanished, and driven together to hell; and evil is the resting place. *Qur'an 3:12*

As for those who disbelieve in our communications, we shall make them enter fire; so oft as their skin are thoroughly burned, we will change them for other skin, that may taste the chastisement. *Qur'an 4:56*

I will cast terror into the hearts of those who disbelieve. Therefore strike off their heads and strike off every fingertip of them. *Qur'an 8:12*

Certainly the above revelations and many more like them in the Qur'an are not peaceful or inspired by a peaceful and benevolent Creator. It is therefore easy to begin to see why our definition of peace is not one that the Qur'an actually follows.

Additionally, our definition of equality of women and of human rights which we hold dear in the West comes into stark contrast and conflict with the definition held by Islam. The status of women in Islam does not allow women to live a peaceful or harmonious existence and certainly the Qur'an does not offer words that would inspire equality for women. According to Islam, a woman is the ward of her father as long as she is in his care and then becomes the ward of her husband when she marries, and when her husband dies she becomes the ward of her son, grandson, and so on, and if she has no male relatives she becomes the ward of her community.[4]

The *Webster's New Word Dictionary* defines "ward" as "a person under the care of a guardian or court." Therefore, according to Islam, a woman never matures, and she must always be under the care of a male relative, a guardian, or Islamic court. I don't consider this respect for women but an insult to womanhood.

Once a Muslim explained to me that this is because women get pregnant and take care of their children; therefore their men should take care of them. This is a wonderful idea for men to take care of their women while they are pregnant or have small children.

However, why should an unmarried woman, a woman who is not pregnant, a grandmother, or an elderly woman be under the care of a guardian? In addition, only people with mental disorders are placed under the care of a court. Women are not crazy or immature; therefore, they don't need to be under court-appointed guardian supervision.

According to Ayatollah Khomeini, the leader of the Iranian Islamic revolution and the past leader of the Shiite Muslims, the Islamic requirement for a judge is that "the person have reached puberty, know Qur'anic laws, be just, not have amnesia, not be a bastard and not be of a female sex."[5]

Therefore, women are not considered mature enough to be able to judge others. This is the reason for not giving women the right to vote in many of the so-called Islamic democracies. What an oxymoron considering half the population of many of these countries cannot get involved in the destiny of their nations. Yet these nations still consider themselves democracies.

It is indeed because of the numerous contradictions within Islam that long before my sister's death I chose to leave the religion I had inherited from my family. I will share something of my journey here to enable you to see why I, like so many of the people you will hear from in this book, chose to leave Islam.

Apparently, or so I was told, I was six days old when my grandfather passed on his religion to me. He did so by reciting a series of Arabic words into my ear. I am quite positive that those were the only Arabic words my grandfather could recite and perhaps he did not understand those words himself. We are Iranian and our language is Persian and a vast majority of the Iranians, including my family, do not speak Arabic, the language of Islam. For Muslims, religion is like the color of our eyes. It is hereditary. Whether you ultimately believe is really not the issue, but it is something you are born with.

For my kindergarten education I was sent to this neighborhood religious school where an old lady named Kobra was its headmistress. I hated this school and the headmistress because she always looked so mean in those black shrouds she covered herself in. She wore black at all times. No laughter, no music, no play—just Allah and Islam. The school was dirty and all the teacher did was read her Qur'an and prayer book. Even at my young age, my instinct suggested to me that she had no education and could not read, a fact confirmed when I would place her Qur'an upside down and she would still read it just the same.

As a child I learned very quickly how differently boys were treated from girls. I wanted to ride a tricycle like the boys did, but I was told that girls don't ride tricycles. When I went to school I wanted to learn how to play the violin, however I was told a good girl does not play musical instruments. When I wanted to ride a bicycle, I was told good girls don't ride bicycles; the same went for riding horses, swimming, and any other activities.

From the time I was a little girl I learned the importance of virginity for a girl in Islamic culture. A girl must be a virgin when she gets married. In addition, the marriage age for a girl is nine years of age. As a matter of fact, Khomeini, the leader of the Islamic Republic of Iran, stated that, "The most suitable time for a girl to get married is the time when the girl can have her first menstrual period in her husband's house rather than her father's."[6] I have learned that this quote originally is from Imam Mosa-e-Kazem, the eighth Imam of Shite—the twelfth sect in Islam—the religion of 98 percent of Iranians. This is the mindset of the Islamic regime.

Luckily my family was not religious; however, the culture of the family and the society we lived in was Islamic. The thought of being married and sent away to a total stranger at age nine used to send shivers down my spine. I watched when the father of the girl who worked for our mother married her off to a man with three sons older than she was. She was just eleven years old, an old maid by her father's standard.

There were also other aspects of Islam which affected me personally. I remember the time when my father had a lamb sacrificed in front of our eyes in our yard. Watching how that poor animal struggled to get himself free and how he moaned and moved his legs and body after his throat was slit made me hate and curse the ritual for which this lamb had to die.

The night following the lamb sacrifice my father's mother, the only religious person in our entire family, told me the story of Abraham and his son Ishmael. She told me how God had asked Abraham to take his son to a place and sacrifice him in order to show his devotion to Al-mighty. And that as he placed the knife over his son's throat he had heard a lamb and then had sacrificed the lamb instead. That was why we had to sacrifice the lamb that morning. The story was quite scary for me. Many nights I had nightmares about this story. I would dream about my father sacrificing me to show his devotion to God and then I would jump and find out I was still alive. I finally convinced myself that God would only ask men to sacrifice their sons and not daughters. After all why should anyone sacrifice a girl? In a way I would feel happy being a girl. My father's mother used to teach me about religion and Islam. She used to tell me, "God is great, knows everything, and has created man and the universe." Then she would ask me to pray in Arabic.

"Grandma, doesn't Allah understand Persian?"

"Well, no. You must speak to Allah in Arabic."

"But you just said Allah made everything. If he made the Persian language, then how come he can't understand it?"

Following these types of arguments during which time Grandma was cornered and did not have an answer to give, I completely discarded religion and Islam. My dislike of religion was reinforced when I started studying *Sharia* in high school. What I learned was so humiliating to women and so oppressive that I even hated to read the book.

I did not understand why divorce was a unilateral right of a man, or why women had to surrender their children to their father's family when their husbands divorced them or when the husband died. Why women inherited half as much as their male siblings and why a boy could do what he pleased and girls were denied all rights. Why we always had to wait for men and boys to finish eating and then we nourished from their leftovers. Why was my body everyone else's property except mine? If I stood at our doorstep and talked to the neighbor boy, every male relative of ours made it his responsibility to force me inside the house. I felt like a prisoner. In fact, the only males I could actually talk to were the ones chosen for me.

Indeed, one of the most disgusting aspects of Islam to me was the process of *khastegary* (matchmaking). In this process, women within a man's immediate or even extended family would search for a suitable girl for their male relative. Each time my family members visited a girl as a potential wife for my uncle or cousins, their evaluation of the poor young girl would make me sick. It was as if they were buying a piece of furniture. The only thing important was her physical features. In addition, she must be a virgin. In the case that a girl's virginity cannot be proven, her parents must pay the groom and his parents for all the wedding costs and the marriage is annulled the next day.

When I was a teenager in Tehran, I went to a relative's wedding. This girl was only fourteen years old. Her parents were so concerned about her virginity that they were practically glued to the newly married couple's bedroom door. They stood there until the groom, a thirty-year-old man, came out of the room. They then entered and removed the bloody sheet from under their raped daughter and with jubilation offered the sheet to the groom's parents as the proof of their daughter's virginity. I never wanted to be treated in that manner on my wedding night.

There are so many laws in Islam that will turn off any educated person completely. Yet we are still told that Islam is a religion of peace. One such law is the Shiite custom of *sigeh*, or temporary marriage. I call it religiously sanctioned prostitution. Marriage in Islam is a contract between a man and a woman's guardian for a specified length of time. It is almost like acquiring leasehold on a property.

In a permanent marriage, a man marries a woman for ninety-nine years because no one is supposed to live that long. In reality, most husbands die way before this period is over since they marry in their late thirties and early forties. Women who have been given away by their guardians when they were quite young get a chance to live alone in peace the rest of their lives. In a temporary marriage, the man specifies the term of the contract. He asks a woman or her guardian if she would marry him for any amount of time from ten minutes to an hour, a week, or some months for a specified amount of money. If she or her guardian agrees to the terms, then they are married and the marriage is annulled when the time has elapsed. In truth, this is a legal way for a man to enjoy the company of the young woman without any long-term commitment.

Another barbaric Islamic law is that of the *mohalel*. A man actually pays another man to marry his three-times-divorced wife for one night, have sex with her, and divorce her the next day so that the husband can remarry his divorced wife. Years ago, one of our distant relatives divorced his wife three times under rage and then was sorry and wanted to get back with her. However, the *mullah* would not remarry them unless she would marry another man and spend a night with this new husband (allowing him to have sex with her) and then be divorced the next day and remarry her ex-husband.

I recall what a circus this was. The ex-husband was desperate to find a man and pay him to marry his mistakenly divorced wife for one night and then divorce her the next day. Since his ex-wife was a very beautiful woman from a distinguished family, the man needed someone he could trust to actually divorce his wife the next day. So finally he asked one of my father's workers to marry the woman. The husband then paid this man a substantial sum of money. The man slept with the husband's wife for one night and they were divorced the next day and the couple was able to get back together. What was appalling to me was that none of the women in the family thought much about the consequences of this one-night stand. Perhaps it was because they had all been raped on their wedding nights by a strange man (arranged marriage) and getting raped again by another strange man (*mohalel*) was not such a big issue. Alternatively, maybe many of them wished that they would be divorced so they could marry another man who would treat them better than their husbands did.

Now that I think about this law, I find it appalling and humiliating to women. In both cases—the first arranged marriages and the one-night stands due to divorce—the women are not consulted and they are forced to accept rape by a total stranger, first because of pressure from their parents, and then due to unspeakable acts by their husbands. Muslim apologists would tell you this law was put in place so men would not divorce their wives three times: a deterrent to divorce. In Islam a man has the unilateral right to divorce (by itself a violation of a woman's human rights), under the following procedures. A man can divorce his wife once, by telling her, "I divorce you," and if they are faced with each other the divorce is nullified and they can resume normal relations. A man can divorce his wife twice—"I divorce you, I divorce you"—and then if they have sexual intercourse the divorce is nullified and they can resume their marital relations. However, a man divorces his wife three times—"I divorce you, I divorce you, I divorce you"—in the presence of a witness. Then, in order for them to get back together, the man has to find a *mohalel*. Many times these *mohalels* do not divorce the wife the next day. Moreover, there is nothing the ex-husband can do about it.

I found this law barbaric and inhumane for the following reasons. First, the woman's feelings and rights are not considered and she is raped for one night by a total stranger. Second, the idea of a man paying another man to ravish his wife for an entire night is appalling. Finally, if the *mohalel* does not divorce the woman, she is forced to live a life in misery (unless the *mohalel* happens to be kinder than her ex-husband is) and away from her children by the first husband, if she had any.

After this circus in the family, I decided that I did not want to be a Muslim; however, I still did not have the courage to leave the faith completely. I left Iran with a small Qur'an in my pocket and passed under a large one coming out of our home on my way to the airport. Even though I had never prayed, fasted, been to a mosque, or performed any religious ritual in my entire life, I still believed in God and his Prophet Mohammad when I left Iran in 1964 to come to the United States of America.

After I learned the English language well enough to read, I read part of the Qur'an in English. I had never read the Qur'an. When I left Iran it was not translated in Persian or perhaps we did not know about it. I read some text of the Qur'an translated into English. I was appalled by such texts as the Surah of Lights, where God supposedly tells Mohammad, "Prophet, tell your wives, daughters, and other women who believe in me to conceal their eyes and their treasures from the sight of stranger" (*Qur'an* 33:59). My problem was to know how far a woman should be dressed to conceal her treasures, and besides, what are a woman's treasures? Was a woman's treasure under her belt or her brain? The way the Muslims in my family and neighborhood acted, it was clear that a woman's treasure was her virginity before marriage and her vagina after marriage. I resented that. Then I read more in the Qur'an and in other books, and after reading all these sayings and proverbs I was convinced that the religion only destroyed a human's ability to think and act on his or her own behalf. I have listed some of these sayings below.

> Your wives are your tillage; go in unto your tillage in what manner so ever you will.

> Good women are obedient, as for those from whom you fear rebellion, admonish them and banish them to beds apart, and scourge them. *Qur'an 2:223*

> I was standing at the edge of fire (hell) and the majority of the people going there were women. *Prophet Mohammad (Sahih Bukhari, Sahih Muslim Volume 4, Book 54, Number 464)*

> It is better to wallow in mud with pigs than to shake the hand of a woman. *An Islamic leader in Indonesia*

> A woman's heaven is beneath her husband's feet. *Islamic saying*

> Women should be exposed to the daylight three times in their lives. When they are born, when they are married and when they die. *Islamic saying*

Later in my research on Islam I learned about the marriage of the Prophet to his first wife when he was twenty-four years old and sixteen years her junior. She was a rich, twice-divorced lady who proposed to Mohammad. Then after she died at age seventy-two, when he was fifty-six years of age, he married a seven-year-old girl. He supposedly had sex with her when she was nine years of age, and pronounced her mother of all Muslims at the time of his death when she was only eighteen years old so that she would never be able to marry another man.

In the last eight to ten years of his life, the Prophet Mohammad married some fifteen to forty-six women. Muslim apologists say that these women were all widows and that they had no place to go and no one to take care of them. So Allah ordered his Prophet to marry them. I find this excuse preposterous. Ayesha, whom

Mohammad married when she was only seven years old, was a child from a very well-to-do household and her father had become a Muslim years before she was born. Zynab was married to the Prophet's adopted son Zayd and was quite happily married until Mohammad asked Zayd to divorce Zynab so Mohammad could marry her himself. In order to get the approval of the Gorish tribe, he brought the excuse that "a Muslim man is not allowed to raise another man's child; therefore, Zayd is not his son, because he adopted Zayd prior to his ordination as a Muslim prophet." That is the main reason adoption is not legal in Islamic countries. In addition, Reyhaneh was a beautiful married woman when her husband was decapitated by the Prophet's bandits and she was taken to the Prophet's bed the same night. These women were not widowed. They indeed had someone to take care of them.

When I read such stories my mind just exploded. How could so many people in this world follow a womanizer and a child molester? How could my grandfather make me a Muslim when I was six days old to be a follower of such a criminal? Then I came to the conclusion that he did not know about it. Alternatively, if he did, it was because he had been raised in such a barbaric culture himself and did not know better.

When my son was born, I did not give him any religion. I did not give him any religious education about God and his prophets. As a matter of fact, I did not mutilate my child, either. My faith in God was totally eroded on April 1, 1979, following the establishment of the Islamic Republic or the government of God, in the country of my birth, Iran—when the country experienced a dramatic return to the Dark Ages due to the establishment of the following Islamic laws. Women were the first victims of the regression. More than 130 years of struggle were repudiated by the medieval religious rulers. Bereaved of their constitutional rights, women were socially reduced to lower individuals and second-rank citizens.

In March 1979, Khomeini employed the *hijab* as a symbol of struggle against imperialism and corruption. He declared that "women should not enter the ministries of the Islamic Republic bareheaded. They may keep on working provided that they wear the *hijab*" (*Kayhan*, March 1979).

The Ministry of Education specified the color and the style of the suited clothing for the girl students (black, straight, and covered from head to toe for children as young as six years of age). To suppress the refractory women, the government set up special units. Patrols controlled whether women observed the Islamic habit on the streets.

The Islamic government went even further. During the last twenty-eight years, women's conditions have continuously deteriorated. Nonetheless, in spite of the tortures (flagellation, stoning, imprisonment, and total segregation), Iranian women have not ceased their worthy struggle.

Under the Islamic rules, the family protection law has been abrogated. Polygamy has been reestablished. The Islamic Republic resolutely supports the practice of polygamy. Under the Islamic Republic, provisional marriage was sanctioned. Consequently, a man may marry four "permanent" and as many "provisional" wives as he desires.

> Most Europeans have mistresses. Why should we suppress human instincts? A rooster satisfies several hens, a stallion several mares. A woman is unavailable during certain periods whereas a man is always active. *Ayatollah Ghomi, Le Monde, January 20, 1979.*

> The specific task of women in this society is to marry and bear children. They will be discouraged from entering legislative, judicial, or whatever careers which may require decision-making, as women lack the intellectual ability and discerning judgment required for theses careers. *Ayatollah Mutahar, (one of the principal ideologues of the Islamic Republic of Iran), on "The Question of Veil," man's testimony is equal to that of two women.*[7]

According to Clauses 33 and 91 of the law in respect, *qisas* (The Islamic Retribution Bill), and its boundaries, the value of a woman witness is considered only half as much as of a man. According to the Islamic Penal Law that is being practiced by the present regime of Iran, "a woman is worth half of a man."

According to Clause 6 of the Law of Retribution and Punishment, "If a woman murders a man his family has the right to a sum paid to the next of kin as compensation for the slaughter of a relative. By contrast, if a man murders a woman, her murderer must, before retribution, pay half the amount of a man's blood money to her guardian."

In 1991, the Prosecutor-General of Iran declared that "anyone who rejects the principle of *hijab* is an apostate and the punishment for an apostate under Islamic law is death."

Girls condemned to the death penalty may not undergo the sentence as long as they are virgin. Thus they are systematically raped before the sentence is executed.

Meanwhile, a report of the Special Representative of the Commission of the Human Rights of the United Nations in the Islamic Republic of Iran, 1992, stated:

> To rape women prisoners, especially virgin girls, who are accused of being against the regime, is a normal and daily practice in the Islamic Republic's prisons, and by doing so, the clergies declare that they adhere to the merits of the Islamic principles and laws, preventing a virgin girl to go to heaven. *Mullahs* believe that these are ungodly creatures and they do not deserve it, therefore they are raped to be sure they will be sent to hell.[8]

Further evidence of the treatment of women is provided in article 115 of the Islamic Constitution that clearly states that the president of the country should be elected out of all God-fearing and dedicated men; this means a woman can neither be president nor possess the rank of *Valiat-e-Faghih* (the religious spiritual leader) or the position of leader of a Muslim nation.

Iranian women are prevented from marrying foreigners unless they obtain a written permission from the Ministry of the Interior. The Ministry of the Interior's Director General for the Affairs of Foreign Citizens and Immigrants, Ahmad Hosseini, stated on March 30, 1991: "Marriages between Iranian women and foreign men will create many problems for these women and their children in the future, because the marriages are not legally recognized. Religious registrations of such marriages will not be considered as sufficient documentation to provide legal services to these families." Also, "Married women are not allowed to travel abroad without presenting a written permission from their husbands."

Additionally, the latest reports of the various international organizations such as Amnesty International and the United Nation's Human Rights Commission give a clear picture of the basic human rights violations that Iranian women, as well as Iranian men and children, are experiencing.

The only thing the Islamic Republic has brought to the Iranian people is poverty and misery. I just wonder why God discards them. At the time of the revolution Khomeini told people that God was on their side. If this is what we will get by having God on our side, I am so pleased to not have Khomeini's so-called "God" on mine.

Parvin Darabi

President, Dr. Homa Darabi Foundation (www.homa.org)

Co-author of *Rage Against the Veil*, Prometheus Books, 1999

CHAPTER TWO

WHY I LEFT ISLAM

"I remember one occasion in Bethlehem when all the viewers in a jam-packed theater clapped their hands with joy as we watched the movie 21 Days in Munich. *The moment we saw the Palestinians...killing the Israeli athletes, we...yelled, '*Allahu akbar!*' A slogan of joy."*

ONE OF THE MOST POWERFUL forces in the world is the testimony of a changed life. Like Parvin and Homa Darabi, Walid Shoebat knows the evils of terrorism because he once lived them—in fact, he practiced them. As a teenager, he bombed a bank in the Holy Land and took part in beating an Israeli soldier. When his Catholic wife later challenged him to study the Bible, his hardened heart began to soften as he studied the grace, reconciliation, and love offered in the sacrifice of Jesus Christ. Today, Walid speaks out about the need for religious tolerance and personal freedom. And his appeal is compelling, given his journey from terrorist to anti-terrorist.

Walid Shoebat's story poignantly shows us what will happen to our own neighborhoods if we don't stop Islamic terrorism. He left Islam for a specific reason: It produced violence. He fears that if we in the West don't stand together now, we will face greater Islamic violence later. Only then, it won't be overseas—it will be in our own communities.

Why I Left Islam

I was born and raised in Beit Sahour, Bethlehem, in the West Bank, to a prominent family. My paternal grandfather was the *muhktar*, or chieftain, of the village. He was a friend of Haj-Ameen Al-Husseni, the Grand Mufti of Jerusalem and notorious friend of Adolf Hitler. My maternal grandfather, F.W. Georgeson, on the other hand, was a great friend of Winston Churchill, and a staunch supporter of the establishment of the state of Israel, though I did not become aware of this until much later in my life. I was born on one of Islam's most holy days, the birthday of the Muslim Prophet Mohammad; this was a great honor to my father. To commemorate this great day, he named me Walid, which relates to the Arabic word *mauled*, meaning "the birth." It was my father's way of memorializing the fact that his son was born on the birthday of the last and greatest of all prophets.

My father was a Palestinian Muslim who taught English and Islamic studies in the Holy Land. My mother was an American who married my father in 1956 during his studies in the United States. Fearing the impact of the American way of life for their two children, while my mother was pregnant with me my parents left to live in Bethlehem, which at that time was part of Jordan. It was 1960. Shortly after my parents arrived in Bethlehem, I was born. As my father changed jobs, we moved to Saudi Arabia and then back to the Holy Land—this time to the lowest place on earth: Jericho. I grew up learning how to hate but was ultimately saved by the loving example of my American mother, who understood compassion, fairness, and freedom.

I cannot forget the first song I learned in school. It was titled "Arabs our Beloved and Jews our Dogs." I was seven years old. I remember wondering at that time who the Jews were, but along with the rest of my classmates, I repeated the words without any real understanding as to their meaning.

As I grew up in the Holy Land, I lived through several battles between the Arabs and the Jews. The first battle, while we were still living in Jericho, was the Six Day War, when the Jews captured old Jerusalem and the rest of "Palestine." It is hard to describe what an immense disappointment and great shame this was to the Arabs and Muslims worldwide.

The American Consul in Jerusalem came to our village just before the war to evacuate all the Americans in the area. Because my mother was an American, they offered us assistance, but my father refused any help from them, because he loved his country. I still remember many things during the war—the noise of the bombing and shelling that went on day and night for six days, the looting of stores and houses by the Arabs in Jericho, people fleeing to cross the Jordan River for fear of the Israelis.

The war was so named because in a mere six days, the Israelis gained victory over a multi-national Arab force which mounted attacks from multiple fronts. On only the seventh day of this battle, Rabbi Shalom Goren, the chief chaplain of the Israeli Defense Forces, let loose a resounding note on the *shofar*, announcing the Jewish control of the Western Wall and the old city of Jerusalem. Many Jews pointed out the obvious parallels of this event to the biblical account of Joshua and the Israelites when they took Jericho. Joshua and the Israelites circled the walls of Jericho for six days, and then on the seventh day, they circled the wall seven times. The priests blew the *shofars* as all the Israelites shouted with one voice. The walls fell and the Israelites took the city.

After the war, to my father in Jericho, it seemed as if the walls had crumbled on him directly. During the war he would sit glued to the radio listening to the Jordanian news station. He used to say that the Arabs were winning the war—but he was listening to the wrong station. The Israeli station was announcing the truth of their imminent victory. Instead my father chose to believe the Arabs who claimed that the Israelis were—as always—lying, promoting false propaganda. How many of us today remember Saddam's information minister, popularly known as "Baghdad Bob," and all of the wild claims and false reports that he was spouting in the few days leading up to the fall of Baghdad? In the Islamic world, it seems as though some things never change.

Later, we moved back to Bethlehem, where my father enrolled us in an Anglican-Lutheran school to take advantage of the superior English courses. My brother, sister, and I were the only Muslims in the school. The three of us were hated. Not so much because we were Muslims, but because we were half American. Although it was a Christian school, it still bore the traits of the Islamicized form of Christianity that infects so many of the Palestinian Christians to this day. In order to get along— and sometimes simply to survive—many Christians in Islamic-dominated countries adopt the hateful attitudes of the Muslims around them towards Israel, America, and the West. Because we were half American, the teachers often beat us while the Christian students laughed.

Eventually, my father transferred me to the government school where I began to grow strong in the faith of Islam. I was taught that one day the fulfillment of an ancient prophecy by the Muslim Prophet Mohammad would come to pass. This prophecy foretold a battle in which the Holy Land would be recaptured for Islam and the elimination of the Jews would take place in a massive final slaughter. This prophecy is found in some of the most sacred books of Islamic traditions known as the *Sahih Hadith*. This particular tradition reads as follows and is in the mindset of all radical Islamists:

> [Mohammad said:] The last hour would not come unless the Muslims will fight against the Jews and the Muslims would kill them until the Jews would hide themselves behind a stone or a tree and a stone or a tree would say: Muslim, or the servant of Allah, there is a Jew behind me; come and kill him; but the tree Gharqad would not say, for it is the tree of the Jews. (*Sahih Muslim Book 041, Number 6985*)

When asked where this slaughter would take place, tradition states that it would be "in Jerusalem and the surrounding area."

During my youth, like my father, I was always attuned to Islam and whatever our Muslim teachers taught us. I, like so many of my classmates, was deeply inspired by Mohammad's dark and bloody vision. I offered my life to *jihad*, or holy war, in order to help fulfill this prophecy. I wanted to be part of the unfolding of Mohammad's grand plan, when Islam would gain the final victory over the Jews and finally—without any further obstacles—rule the world. This was the ideology of my mentors, and while I have left this school of fanaticism behind, millions of people in the Middle East still believe it, and they still fight to make it a reality.

During my early teenage years, there were often riots at school against what we called the Israeli occupation. Whenever I could, I assumed the role of agitator and instigator. I vowed to fight my Jewish enemy, believing that in doing so, I was doing God's will on the earth. I remained true to those vows as I raged against the Israeli army in every riot I could. I used any means available to inflict maximum damage and harm. I rioted in school, on the streets, and even on the Temple Mount in Jerusalem. Throughout high school, I was one of the leading activists for the cause of Islam. I would prepare speeches, slogans, and write anti-Israeli graffiti in an effort to provoke other students to throw rocks at the armed Israeli soldiers. The thundering echoes of our dark chants still reverberate in my memory:

> No peace or negotiations with the enemy!
>
> Our blood and our souls we sacrifice to Arafat!
>
> Our blood and our souls we sacrifice to Palestine!
>
> Death to the Zionists!

My dream was to die as a *shaheed*, a martyr for Islam. At demonstrations I would open my shirt hoping to be shot, but because the Israelis would never shoot at the body, I never succeeded. When school pictures were taken, I would purposefully pose with a grim face anticipating that it was my turn to be in the paper as the next martyr. Many times I came close to being killed during youth protests and clashes with the Israeli army. My heart was resolute; nothing could take away my drive—my hatred and anger—other than a miracle. I was one of those young men that you might have seen on CNN hurling rocks and Molotov cocktails during the days of the *Intifada* or "the uprising." At the time, I would have resented the label; but the simple truth is that I was a young budding terrorist. The Islamo-Nazi brainwashing of my teachers and *imams*—of my entire culture—was having its desired effect.

What I now know is that I was not only terrorizing others, but in many ways, I was terrorizing myself by what I believed. My ultimate fight was to gain enough merit—to build up a solid track record of terror—in order to earn Allah's favor. I lived in fear of judgment and hell and thought that only by behaving as I did would I ever have a chance at making it into *janna* (paradise, or heaven). I was never confident that my "good deeds" would outweigh my bad deeds on the scale on the Day of Judgment. I was driven by not only anger and hatred, but also spiritual insecurity and fear. I believed what I was taught: the surest way to ease Allah's anger towards my sins was to die fighting the Jews. Perhaps, if I were successful, I would even be rewarded with a special place in heaven where beautiful wide-eyed women would fulfill my most intimate desires.

It's hard to convey the degree to which someone like me, growing up under the Palestinian education system, is brain-washed. Every voice in authority speaks the same message: the message of Islam—*jihad* or hatred of the Jews—and things that no young mind should ever be subjected to.

I remember an occasion at Dar-Jaser High School in Bethlehem during Islamic studies when some of my classmates asked the teacher if it was permitted for Muslims to rape the Jewish women after we defeated them. His response was, "The women captured in battle have no choice in this matter; they are concubines and they need to obey their masters. Having sex with slave captives is not a 'matter of choice for slaves'." This was not merely the opinion of the teacher, but is clearly taught in the Qur'an:

> Forbidden to you also are married women, except those who are in your hand as slaves, this is the law of Allah for you. *Qur'an 4:24*

And elsewhere it says:

> O prophet; we allowed thee thy wives to whom thou hast paid their dowries, and the slaves whom thy right hand pos-seseth out of the booty which Allah hath granted thee, and the daughters of thy uncle, and of thy maternal aunt, who fled with thee to Medina, and any believing woman who hath given herself up to the prophet, if the prophet desired to wed her, a privilege to thee above the rest of the faithful. *Qur'an 33:50*

We had no problem with Mohammad taking advantage of this privilege as he married around fourteen wives for himself and had several slave girls from the booty that he collected as a result of his victorious battles. We really never knew how many wives he had and that question was always a debatable issue to us. One of these wives was even taken from his own adopted son Zayd. After Zayd married her, Mohammad took interest. Zayd offered her to Mohammad, but it was not until a revelation came down from Allah that Mohammad generously accepted Zayd's offer. Others of Mohammad's wives were Jewish captives forced into slavery after Mohammad beheaded their husbands and families. These were the things we learned about in our Islamic Studies course in high school. This was the man that we were supposed to emulate in every way. This was our Prophet, and it was from him and his sayings that we learned to hate Jews.

I remember one occasion in Bethlehem when all the viewers in a jam-packed theater clapped their hands with joy as we watched the movie *21 Days in Munich*. The moment we saw the Palestinians throwing grenades into the helicopter and killing the Israeli athletes, we all—hundreds of viewers—yelled, "*Allahu akbar!*" A slogan of joy.

In an attempt to change the hearts of Palestinians, the Israeli TV station would show Holocaust documentaries. I would sit and watch, cheering the Germans while I ate popcorn. My heart was so hardened, it was impossible for me to change my attitudes toward the Jews; only a "heart transplant" would do that job.

By the grace of God, I had something that very few of my classmates had. I had a mother who was a compassionate and contrarian voice—patiently trying to reach me in the midst of the deafening cacophony of hatred that surrounded me. She would try to teach me at home about what she called "a better plan." However, it had little effect on me at the time, for my resolve was solid—I would live or die fighting against the Jews. But a mother never gives up.

I didn't know it at the time, but my mother had been influenced by an American missionary couple. She had even asked them to secretly baptize her. However, when she refused to be baptized in a pond full of green algae, the missionary priest had to plead to the YMCA in Jerusalem to clear the pool of men, and my mother was then baptized. No one from our family knew.

Many times my mother would take me on trips to various museums in Israel. This had a very positive effect on me and I fell in love with archeology. I was fascinated with it. In my many arguments with her, I would directly tell her that the Jews and Christians had changed and corrupted the Bible. Her response was to take me to the Scroll Museum in Jerusalem where she showed me the very ancient scroll of Isaiah—still intact. My mother made some of her most effective points using no words at all. Despite my mother's patient and gentle attempts to reach me, I was unreachable. I would torment her with insults. I would call her an "infidel" who claimed that Jesus was the Son of God and a "damned American imperialist." I would show her pictures in the newspaper of all the Palestinian teenagers who had been "martyred" as a result of clashing with the Israeli soldiers and I would demand that she give an answer. I hated her and many times I asked my father to divorce her and remarry a good Muslim woman.

Despite all of this, it was my mother—when I was thrown in the Muscovite Prison in Jerusalem—who went to the American Consulate in Jerusalem to try to get me out. The Muscovite Prison was a Russian compound that served as Jerusalem's central prison for those who were caught inciting violence against Israel. My dear mother was so worried over the direction that my life was taking that her hair started to fall out. Her worries were not unfounded. During my time in jail I was initiated into Yasser Arafat's Fatah terror group. Soon after, I was recruited by a well-known bomb maker from Jerusalem named Mahmoud Al-Mughrabi.

The time had come for more than mere protests and riots. Al-Mughrabi and I arranged to meet on Bab-El-Wad Street at the Judo-Star Martial Arts Club run by his father near the Temple Mount in Jerusalem. He gave me a very sophisticated explosive device that he had personally assembled. I was supposed to use the bomb—an explosive charge hidden in a loaf of bread—to blow up the Bank Leumi branch in Bethlehem. Mahmoud helped me smuggle the bomb, as did the Muslim Wakf—the religious police on the Temple Mount. From the Temple Mount, I walked out onto the platform with explosives and a timer in my hand. We walked along the walls and avoided all of the checkpoints. From there, I walked to the bus station and took a bus to Bethlehem. I was fully ready to give my life if I had to. I stood before the bank and my hand was literally ready to pitch the bomb at the front doors, when I saw some Palestinian children walking near the bank. At the last moment, I threw the bomb instead on the bank's rooftop. And I ran. As I reached the Church of the Nativity, I heard the explosion. I was so scared and so depressed that I couldn't sleep for days. I was only sixteen years old. I wondered if I had killed anyone. That was the first time I came to grips with what it would be like having blood on my hands. I didn't enjoy what I had done, but I felt compelled to do it because it was my duty.

It is also with difficulty that I recall to you this next story. It was my first attempt to lynch a Jew. Like swarms of locusts, stones were flying everywhere as we clashed with the Israeli soldiers. A group of us had set fire to a row of tires to use as a blockade. One soldier was hit with a rock. He chased after the kid who had hit him. Instead we caught the soldier. Like a pack of wild animals, we attacked him with everything we had. I had a club and I used it to pound him in the head until the club broke. Another teenager had a stick with a nail sticking out. He kept whacking the poor young man's skull until he was covered with blood. We nearly killed him. Incredibly, as if with a final burst of adrenaline, he lunged across the blockade of burning tires and escaped to the other side where the other Israeli soldiers carried him to safety. From where he found the strength I do not know. But I think how glad I am now that he ran. Now, these many years later, it is hard for me to express how deeply it grieves me that I ever committed such acts. I am not the same person that I was in those days.

After I graduated from high school, my parents sent me to the United States to seek a higher education. I enrolled at what was then called the Loop College, located in the heart of downtown Chicago. When I arrived, I immediately became involved with many anti-Israeli social and political events. I still sincerely believed that the day was coming when the whole world would submit to Islam and then the whole world would realize just how much she owed the Palestinian people for all of their losses as the vanguard in the Islamic war against Israel.

The Loop College was full of various Islamist organizations. When I walked into the cafeteria, it was almost like walking into an Arab café in the Middle East. Various Islamist groups operated out of the school in those days, each competing for the recruitment of the other students. I immediately began devoting my energies to serving as an activist for the PLO—the Palestinian Liberation Organization. I was supposed to be officially working as an interpreter and counselor for Arab students through an American program called CETA (Comprehensive Employment and Training Act) in which I was paid by grants from the United States government. The truth, however, is that much of what I did involved interpreting advertisements for events whose goal it was to win American sympathy for the Palestinian cause. Actually, "win sympathy" may be a rather misleading expression. We were attempting to brainwash the Americans—all of whom we viewed as being incredibly gullible. In Arabic, the advertisements for these events would openly use *jihadist*, anti-Semitic descriptions such as: "There will be rivers of blood... Come and support us to send out students to Southern Lebanon to fight the Israelis..." The English versions of the signs, on the other hand, would utilize fluffy and innocuous descriptions such as: "Middle Eastern cultural party, come and join us, we will be serving free lamb and baklava..." That was 1970.

Then came Black September. Black September is the month known throughout the Middle East as the time when King Hussein of Jordan moved to quash an attempt by the PLO in Jordan to overthrow his monarchy. Many Palestinians were killed during the conflict, which lasted for almost a year until July of '71. The end result of all this was the expulsion of the PLO and thousands of Palestinians from Jordan into Lebanon.

Of course, the conflict spilled over and affected the various Arab student organizations at the Loop College. It was very disheartening and frustrating for me to watch, as I knew that without unity, the cause of Islam—the cause of the *jihad* in America—would get nowhere. It was at this time that I joined Al-Ikhwan—the Muslim Brotherhood.

The Muslim Brotherhood is a father organization to dozens of other terrorist organizations throughout the world. I was not alone in joining the Brotherhood, either; there were hundreds of other Muslim students from all over the United States that also joined in those days. I believed that working as an activist for the Muslim Brotherhood was the best way to help bring about a much-needed unity among Muslims; not Palestinian Muslims or Jordanian Muslims, but rather one Muslim *ummah*—one universal Islamic community—under the one umbrella of Islam. To this end, a Jordanian *sheikh* named Jamal Said came to the United States to recruit students. The recruitment meetings were held in basements or rented hotel rooms. Muslim students flocked from all over the U.S. to attend the meetings and listen to Sheikh Jamal Said. Jamal had an almost legendary status and reputation. He was an associate of Abdullah Azzam, who is famous throughout the Middle East for being the mentor of none other than Osama bin Laden.

People often ask me if I think that there are terrorist cells operating within the United States. There can be no question that there are. While so many of America's college students in the '70s were experimenting with drugs, protesting their government, and participating in the birth of the "flower child" movement, they were oblivious to the other underground revolution that was being birthed by radical Muslim students across the country. Within Islam, it is taught that when the Muslims enter a country to conquer it for Allah, there are various stages to that "invasion" if you will. Those were the early stages of the most subversive movement that this country will ever know. It was the birth of the *jihadist* movement in America.

I eventually moved to California, where I met my wife, a Catholic from Mexico. I wanted to convert her to Islam. I told her the Jews had corrupted the Bible and she asked me to show her some examples of this corruption. She issued me a challenge: She challenged me to study the Bible for myself to see if indeed all of the things that I had been taught about the Bible and the Jews were true or not. Thus began a radical life-changing journey. At this point I had to go and buy a Bible and I started reading it and it had the word "Israel" all over it. The very word I hated was throughout the book. I thought, *how do you explain this?* I started thinking the Jews really didn't do us any harm but we hated them and accused them of this horrible stuff.

This was a journey that for a time, until I found resolution to my questions, was an obsession. I would stay up late at night and read, poring through the Jewish and Christian Scriptures. I read the Old Testament and the New. I studied Jewish history. I prayed and I wrestled with all of the things that I was discovering. Many of my beliefs that formed the very foundations of my Islamic worldview were beginning to crumble. Confronted with the obvious conflict between the worldview and the religion of my youth and the piercing quality of the Bible, I prayed to God for guidance. In the mid-1990s, I went to a family reunion in southern California where a row broke out after I defended the biblical matriarch Rachel, whom my uncle had called a "Jewish whore."

"You deserve to be spat at," my uncle said, and they threw me out of the house.

I realized they knew nothing about history; all they knew was the same propaganda that I had been taught.

My convictions led me to renounce violence and convert to Christianity, but it was at a price: My family disowned me and my own brother threatened to kill me for abandoning Islam. Now I hope that by speaking the truth I will open other people's eyes.

Today, I am the founder of the Walid Shoebat Foundation. My life mission and driving passion is to bring the truth about the Jews and Israel to the world, all the while allowing Christ to bring healing to my own soul through repentance and the pursuit of reconciliation. I have set out to untiringly bring the cause of Israel to hundreds of thousands of people throughout the world. I thank God for giving me the opportunity to seek forgiveness and reconciliation from the Jewish people everywhere throughout the world. To anyone who will listen, I tell my story. In addition, despite numerous threats to my life—including a $10 million bounty issued against me—I continue to speak out against the hatred and the Islamo-Nazi lies that I was indoctrinated under. Until they come for me, I will continue to speak out. Yes, today I say to the whole world, *I love Jews!* And I truly believe that the Jews are God's chosen people whose purpose is to give light to Arabs and to the whole world—if only we would allow them.

Knowing this truth has transferred my way of thinking from being a follower of Mohammad and idolizing Adolf Hitler to believing in Jesus Christ, from believing lies to knowing the truth, from being spiritually sick to being healed, from living in darkness to seeing the light, from being damned to being saved, from doubt to faith, from hate to love, and from evil works to God's grace through Christ. This is who I am today. Praise be to God! I hope in reading my testimony and the others included in this book you may begin to realize that this is a battle between good and evil and peace and terrorism, a clash between freedom and neo-fascism. As I declared while speaking at Columbia University: Today I stand for the rights of all people; I stand for blacks to be free from slavery, for Muslims to freely convert to Christianity, for Jews to refuse to be Christians, and for atheists to have the right to be atheists. And I will die for everyone's right to free speech in the United States.

Walid Shoebat
Founder of the Walid Shoebat Foundation
Author of *Why I Left Jihad* and *Why We Want to Kill You*

CHAPTER THREE

REDEMPTION

"I had always despised the smiles they [Christians] had on their faces when we criticized, hurt, or humiliated them...Now I know the reason for their smiles. It is their love, forgiveness, and tolerance toward their enemies. It is the Christian characteristic of making peace."

WHILE THE TYRANNICAL and extremist elements that exist in Iran and Palestine may not be too surprising to Westerners—especially after September 11—what is happening in neighboring Egypt is. The land of the pharaohs, a must-see destination for millions of tourists, is also, sadly, a hotbed of Islamic extremism.

Egypt is, after all, the location that birthed Osama bin Laden's second in command, Ayman Al-Zawahiri. Though born into the Egyptian aristocracy and trained as a surgeon, Zawahiri, like so many other young men in Egypt, rejected his privileged background and instead grew attracted to radical Islam through the teachings of Sayyid Qutb, the man whose ideas would help shape al-Qaeda. In 1998, Zawahiri brought his Egyptian Islamic Jihad organization into a union with the forces of Osama bin Laden. Together, they formed al-Qaeda and the rest is tragic history. This is the backdrop for the story of Ahmed Awny Shalakamy.[1]

Today, Ahmed believes he is living witness that twisted belief systems inspire humans to commit unthinkable atrocities. He admits that when he was young, he was so filled with hate that he went out with a machete and killed two innocent Sikhs—a father and son. An innocent Bangladeshi Hindu meanwhile, was caught on the street, dragged by Ahmed to a mosque, and beaten to death. The victim's pleas for mercy seemingly had no effect on the fundamentalist worshippers who proceeded to chant "Kill the *kafir!*" In this testimony, Ahmed also reveals how he lured non-Muslim women into Islam, and following their conversion paraded them through the streets to bring shame to their families.

Ahmed has gone through a complete 180-degree turn in his mindset and writes his testimony because he has come to believe humans are not born evil but become evil through indoctrination. He now spends his life finding the women he converted and helping them rebuild the lives he once played a part in shattering.

Ahmed has a message for everyone reading his words: terrorism is not a way of life, but a path to death. And until we stop radical Islam, no one is safe. Ahmed left Islam because he believes it led him to kill. And he worries that Westerners won't recognize this threat until it's too late.

Redemption

I grew up in Giza, Egypt. My father was a building contractor and was involved in Islamic activities. He was the chairman of one of the local Islamic associations and was responsible for making the call for prayer. He also gave Islamic lessons and at times spoke at the mosque on Fridays.

My father hated Christians. He taught me that they are infidels who contradict themselves by saying that Jesus Christ is God while their distorted book (the Bible) has verses that prove he is only a prophet. It was all part of the rhetoric we got used to hearing from booming mosque loudspeakers, and from the playing of radio and audiocassettes in the streets. In such an atmosphere, a Muslim child in Egypt is breastfed hatred along with his mother's milk.

My father's association was active in many fields. It ran a dormitory for girls, a workshop, a clinic, a nursery, a *madrassah* to study the Qur'an, and a section for preaching Islam. The main interest of his association was to proselytize Islam by any means.

During the rule of the late president Anwar El Sadat, the Grand Imam of El Azhar, Mohammad Abdel Halim Mahmoud, was involved in plotting together with Sadat's vice president, Mr. Hussein el Shafei. Sheikh Keshk was also involved in this planning together with Mohammad Osman Ismail, Assiut's previous governor, and Mohammad Abdel Mohsen Saleh. Both Ismail and Saleh were the founding fathers of the various Islamic proselytizing associations that sprouted up, and with which my father was involved.

The goal of these groups was to convert Egypt into an Islamic state over a period of fifty years. Members of the royal Saudi family, who were related to the Wahabi movement and to oil princes from the Gulf, financed this plan. Money was spent lavishly to seduce Christian women and girls any way possible. The cost in the seventies and early eighties was about five thousand Egyptian pounds for the entrapment of each girl. The money was split so that the Muslim man who lured the Christian woman into conversion received half and the members of the police and collaborating associations would receive the other half.

The work of the proselytizing associations in Egypt continues to take place and the payments for deceptive conversions are now higher. Today the average payment for an ordinary girl is ten thousand Egyptian pounds and payments can be as high as two hundred thousand Egyptian pounds if the girl is from a well-known Christian family, or is the daughter of a university professor, a deputy minister, or related to someone from the clergy.

Like my father, I, too was involved with a proselytizing association. After we succeeded in converting a Christian woman, we would antagonize the Christians by parading the converted girl through the streets. We played loud music and waved flags while shouting "*Allah Akbar*" to declare the victory of Islam. We would also chant slogans to shame the Christians. No Christian would stand in the way of these parades, which were safeguarded by the police.

This was a normal practice until 1985, when such parades were banned. Nevertheless, we continued in our campaign to convert Christian women. We were focused on converting Christian girls and women because we believed this was a greater form of humiliation for Christians. In the East, a man's honor is in his daughter, sister, or wife, and so disgracing any of them is the ultimate humiliation for him.

We used all kinds of tricks to get Christian women. We primarily sought to appeal to their emotions and impulses. We would also get these women involved in moral scandals and use that to coerce them to do whatever we wanted. This is what I did while I was involved with a proselytizing association. Besides receiving payment for this work, I was convinced I received an additional reward because each time I caused a Christian woman to convert to Islam I would be awarded with an acre of land in heaven.

The following accounts are of the women that I lured into Islam through deceptive methods.

Fatima was originally from Cairo and went to college in the city where my family lived. I was in my first year of college at the time, and this was my first case of proselytizing.

She was very pretty. She had a few Muslim girlfriends who told me that she was an easy catch. They arranged for me to meet her and I practiced pretending that I was madly in love, staring at her with desire and faking a quivering voice.

When Fatima and I first started talking, I asked her some questions about the Christian faith. I realized I had to change my tactics if I was going to trap her. I started to convince her that I loved her and I worked on her until she fell for me. Her girlfriends were aware of what was happening and helped me by talking to her about my love for her. I told her that we could marry and keep our different faiths, as Islam allows Muslims to marry the People of the Book because they believe in God. I had my way with her and she became pregnant.

I secretly went to church with her a few times and I even bought Christian books, icons, and the fellowship bread to convince her that I was an admirer of Christianity. I told her that I would have gladly converted to Christianity, but could not do it because I would be killed. I then told her that I loved her and could not live without her and if she converted to Islam, she would not be killed, as she was carrying our baby — the fruit of our love.

She was scared and did not know what to do. At that time, I asked her not to sever her relation with the church, to act as she normally would, and as a camouflage go to church on Thursday for confession, on Friday for communion, and again on Sunday for Mass. She followed my instructions and one day, as per my instructions, she arrived with her suitcase and gold jewelry, and we spent the night at my home in Gameat El Dewal El Arabia

Street. On Saturday morning, she had an appointment with the person in charge at El Azhar. I arranged for her escape to the city where she attended college and where I lived until she finished her studies. I then had her name changed to Fatima El Zahra Mohammad Ali El Mahdi.

The efforts of her family and other Christians to take her back were in vain. I made sure she was the one who adamantly refused to go back after my colleagues and I brainwashed her. My efforts were successful as she became completely convinced that she was now worshipping the true God of Islam.

After five weeks of achieving this victory for Islam and receiving my financial reward, I decided that I did not want to keep this faithless whore as my wife. She was cheap to me and was merely an object for sensual pleasure. *How could I have a son with her who has in him the blood of those Christian infidels*, I reasoned. I ordered her to have an abortion and I used my legitimate right to beat her. I also obliged her to work for her food. I told her she had to serve her Muslim masters who put a roof over her head and she had to be grateful that I married her and saved her from her shame.

I started to think about repeating the same game again with other women, so that I could serve my life, my religion, and my afterlife. I believed by doing this I would serve my religion by making the infidels embrace Islam; I would serve my life by getting financial rewards; and I would serve my afterlife by having many acres written in my name in heaven. I would also have a housecleaner for free. She would work for her food and when I wanted to use her for pleasure, she would be my *odalisque*.

I enjoyed hurting, beating, and humiliating Fatima. I was positive she did not truly convert to Islam and that she was only surrendering to her female instincts. All this made me more inclined to take revenge on her. Fatima stayed with me for three years, seven months, and twelve days. During those three years, seven months, and twelve days that Fatima stayed with me, I made eight girls convert to Islam.

When I met Abir, she was studying in a college located one and a half hours from her home. She came from a wealthy family. Her father and mother were physicians and her brothers were physicians in the Egyptian armed forces. Though she was a churchgoer, she was not religious. Abir was outgoing in her friendships with both Muslims and Christians. Despite her congeniality, we did not find it easy to get to her and had to resort to foul play. As Muslim men, we believed we were in a perpetual war with the "filthy infidels," and therefore it was okay to trick them.

One day I received a visit from a young Muslim man who told me he wanted to marry Abir and asked me to help him convince her to convert to Islam. After much planning, I found out that this girl's best friend was a religious Muslim. However, she still considered the Christian girl her sister and I was disturbed by this. So I paid a visit to the Muslim girl and talked to her about the corrupt beliefs of Christianity and reminded her of what Allah says in the Qur'an: "Ye believers do not take Jews and Christians as friends and those who befriend them are from them, as Allah does not show the right path to the unjust" (Qur'an 5:51). I told her that jihad against them is the duty of every Muslim and she should contribute to the victory of Islam. The Muslim girl was convinced that I was right and asked what was required of her. I told her not to show hatred toward her Christian friend, but to treat her as usual and even try to strengthen their friendship and follow all of my instructions.

I then went to a Muslim pharmacist who is a member of our association and asked him for a drug to induce hallucinations. I told him why I needed the drug. He told me he wanted to contribute to the victory of Islam and therefore he agreed to provide it. I then gave the drug to the Muslim girl and told her to dissolve two tablets in a glass of milk and give it to Abir to drink, and then call us as soon as she noticed any changes in the girl.

The Muslim girl called us as soon as Abir started to hallucinate and lose control in her apartment. When my friend and I arrived, we had a camera and a video recorder. We started joking with Abir and she was responding, not realizing what we were doing until my friend managed to strip her of her clothes and took her to the bedroom.

I recorded everything on video and took pictures for about three hours. When Abir came around, she realized what had happened and started screaming and crying. She insulted us, Islam, and the Prophet of Islam, and tried to tear up the Qur'an, which was with her girlfriend. I showed her the videotape and the photos and threatened to make copies and distribute them to her family, as well as to other Christian families. I reminded her that she would be humiliated by the scandal. She cried and fell to the ground, kissing our shoes and pleading with us not to do this, but we insisted that she had to do whatever we told her to do, as she knew her brothers and relatives might even kill her if they were to see that video.

She gave in. Her tears and desperation made me ecstatic. Over the next few weeks, she accompanied us to the association where she was brainwashed by the *sheikhs*. She could not argue with anything they said. She was miserable and never stopped crying.

We taught her what to say before it was time for her to go to the police department. She followed our instructions when she was interviewed by the police. And when a police officer asked her why she wanted to convert to Islam, she said that the Prophet Mohammad came to her in a dream and greeted her with the Islamic greeting, calling her "Aisha." Jesus was also in the dream, greeted her with the Islamic greeting, and denounced all Christians, saying there is no God but Allah. She said that Jesus told her that he is Allah's slave and prophet and Mohammad is Allah's Prophet. Then, she said, Jesus kissed Mohammad's head and asked her to repeat after him Allah's words from the Qur'an, "Those who believe in any other religion but Islam, Allah will not accept it from them in the end, and they will be losers" (*Qur'an 3:83-85*).

She not only said this in front of the police officers, but also to her family members and the priests who came to visit her. Her reactions during these visits, which were called counseling sessions, were staged by us and agreed on by the police before the meetings. It was all a fraud and though she was visited by different priests, she could only tell them what we had coached her to say.

After all the legal procedures were completed, we got her new identification and a new Islamic name: Aisha Abdalla Elmahdy. We had achieved our plan and the Muslim man, Yasser, a *mujahid*, got the girl he desired along with his financial reward, which was quite hefty because she was from a prominent Christian family. I received twenty-five percent of his share, plus my share of the amount I paid to the collaborating persons involved.

Aisha's family was dishonored and humiliated. As a result, her mother sold her pharmacy and her father sold his clinic. They moved to a place where they could disappear in the crowd and flee the scandal.

So Aisha married Yasser and lived as an outcast, because she was despised by her in-laws. She was married for two months when Yasser said he had had enough of her and did not want to keep her anymore. He divorced her and threw her out into the street.

Since she was our sister in Islam and cannot be homeless, I took her to the association, where she lived and worked as a maid, cleaning the clinic for her food and board. She stayed there for three months until she was legally allowed to remarry. The groom-to-be was a Muslim who knew her story. He was a coolie and was already married with six children. During the day, he labored in the maintenance workshops of the governorate administration. Aisha did not want to marry him and begged us not to allow her to go through with it. We ignored her, and she was forced to marry a man she did not like.

She lived in misery. She worked as a maid to clean homes and sold vegetables in order to feed her husband and his children. It was impossible to imagine that she was once a college student from a wealthy family of physicians. Her life was ruined. Her second husband divorced her after five months. Since she had been married twice she did not remarry and because many had found out about the videotapes and photos taken of her when she was drugged, she was considered unclean. She became homeless and had to spend the night in emergency camps where she lived in sub-human conditions. As she hit bottom she cried: "God have mercy on me."

God showed mercy and answered her prayer.

During the time she was homeless, I became a Christian and was looking for the girls I tricked into converting to Islam. I found out what had become of her and went to visit her with my wife, who had returned to the Church. My wife and I offered to take care of her in our home. We sought to inform her parents about her situation, so I sent a relative of my wife together with a priest, who talked to them. They all cried at the news and expressed their desire to see her. The family reunion was arranged in one of the churches in Cairo. It was an impressive reunion. Though I expected the parents to chastise her, they didn't and were happy to see her.

As her family hugged and kissed her, I was so touched by the love I saw that I wondered why we were hurting Christians the way we did. I had always despised the smiles they had on their faces when we criticized, hurt, or humiliated them. I used to tell myself that they were smiles of malice because they were a minority and could not stand up to us Muslims. Now I know the reason for their smiles. It is their love, forgiveness, and tolerance toward their enemies. It is the Christian characteristic of making peace.

After Abir met her family, she went back home with them. They welcomed her with love and kindness as the scripture says in the story about the prodigal son. Her mother bought her beautiful clothes and her father bought her jewelry. They celebrated her coming home and repeated the words of the Bible ("Our daughter was dead and now is alive and was lost and is now found").

A request was submitted to the Clerical Council to endorse her return to Christianity, which was approved. A Christian lawyer volunteered to petition the court to give her back her Christian name and identity card. The court ruled in her favor. She now lives in France, where she serves in the Coptic Church with her husband and daughter.

CHAPTER FOUR

THE REAL FACE OF ISLAM

"On September 11, 2001, I saw the real face of Islam. I saw the happiness on the faces of our people because so many infidels were slaughtered so easily...I saw many people who started thanking Allah for this massacre."

O N SEPTEMBER 11," Khaled says, "I saw the real face of Islam." On September 11, fifteen of the nineteen hijackers who attacked the United States were Saudi Arabian citizens. Additionally, Osama bin Laden—the chief suspect in the World Trade Center and Pentagon attacks that killed more than three thousand people—was also Saudi-born, though stripped of his citizenship in 1994 by the government. So what about Saudi Arabia enables some of its citizens to feel compelled to embark on suicide missions on the other side of the world? Khaled Waleed believes what he was taught in his mosque in Saudi Arabia is exactly the same teaching that bin Laden received and that is why so many young Muslims in Saudi Arabia support him. Khalid believes that September 11 demonstrated the real face of Islam as taught in the Kingdom. His testimony invites us into a clearer understanding of those teachings and the mindset of the September 11 masterminds. Khalid experienced firsthand the teachings of Islam. He does not believe a few terrorists are distorting the real meaning. He believes terrorists' actions are consistent with Islam. That's why he left. That's why he warns us to stand up to Islam. That's why he fears for the future of the West.

Khalid's Testimony

When I was a child, I used to go to the mosque every day. I used to go there for praying, reciting the Qur'an, reading *ahadith*, and studying *tafseer*.

Our teacher and other Islamic scholars told us that as Muslims, we are the best people in the world. We were also told that Saudi Arabian Muslims are the only true Muslims in the world, and as such, the world must follow us (the Saudi Muslims). Without any question, we steadfastly believed our Islamic scholars and wondered why, despite such exhortations, the world by and large does not emulate us.

We were so proud of being the true Muslims.

Now, I take this to be a lie.

Readers, I would vouch that what I studied in my mosque is exactly what bin Laden studied. You could unmistakably say he is an ideal Muslim. Believe me, almost all our people (in Saudi Arabia) support him and love him very dearly.

We can't blame bin Laden for this; instead, we should blame Islam, the religion of bin Laden. He is simply following his religion to the letter. He is, without doubt, a true Muslim.

My story of leaving Islam started when I was in grade five. I read in *Surah al-kahf, ayat 86 (18:86)* that when Zu-Alqarnain had reached the point of the setting of the sun, he found many people there suffering from the intense heat. This was because they were so close to the sun. The same thing happened to him during the rising of the sun.

I started thinking: *The earth is not flat; it is almost like a ball, so how could he reach the edge of the earth?* I asked my teacher this question. He was confused with my question. He didn't give any answer. He told me just to believe what the Qur'an says.

This was the beginning of my suspicion about the truth in the Qur'an.

Then I had a huge surprise when I found that if I wanted to be a good Muslim I must keep away from non-Muslims. A greater surprise for me was when I discovered that loving any non-Muslims would make me a *kafir* (nonbeliever).

Along with many other activities, I liked going to movies, listening to music, and making friends with athletes and singers— most of whom are non-Muslims. That meant I actually had become a *kafir*. I was taught that, to be in Paradise, I must unconditionally love the Prophet Mohammad, whom I had never seen, more than anyone else, or I will surely go to hell. I became so perplexed.

I listened to my *imams* and was disturbed when they used abusive language to describe the non-Muslims as the grandsons of monkeys and pigs. I thought if anyone commits a sin, this should not be our problem; Allah, in due course, will punish him/her. Why do our *imams* have to condemn these people in such a derogatory manner?

To my surprise, many of my Muslim friends and our *imams* told me that it was my duty to revile and ridicule the non-Muslims, since they are the enemies of Muslims. When I refused to abide by the Islamic tenet of deriding the *kafirs*, they labeled me as a weak Muslim. They even informed me that a Muslim stranger is better than an old trusted *kafir* friend is.

However, I was adamant with my questions—I would not let them go unanswered. The most pertinent question on my mind was: *How could a "God," who claims himself to be filled with mercy, at the same time ask his people to hate one another? Why does "God" have to threaten to burn and torture people who do not believe in him? Is he really that needy? Is it so important that we consistently worship him?*

I started thinking very deeply. I searched the Qur'an and found that everyone's destiny had already been decided by God. God had already determined who will be in hell and who will be in Paradise! Therefore, logically, there is no need for humans to pray. When I put this question to my devoutly religious friends, they became angry. They asked me how I could know in advance whether I should be in hell or in Paradise. I told them that since our destiny has already been ascertained by God, praying or not praying would not really make any difference.

They thought I was crazy since I had developed doubt about Allah and the Qur'an.

This was the start of my hating Islam. However, I was help-less. In the society in which I live I was not able to do anything openly which goes against Islam.

In 1999, my mother fell sick and eventually died. This was a turning point in my life. I thought: *We, the Muslims, are not really the best in the world. Just like any other human being, we too get ill and die, after all.* I also came to the conclusion that if we worked hard we should be successful; if we did not, we are bound to fail. There is no such thing as "Allah's will." There is nothing so special for the Muslims.

When I look around the Islamic world, all I find is utter injustice, unabated discrimination against women and *kafirs,* and blatant abuse and violation of human rights, not to mention the absolute political corruption in Islamic countries. In fact, there is nothing good in our Islamic world to talk about. Most of the Islamic world is in deep trouble, whereas there is relative peace, prosperity, and freedom in most non-Islamic countries.

I asked myself, "What is the reason for this?" The only plausible answer to me was Islam.

Although my hatred of Islam increased, I was unable to leave it. I still could not bring myself to the reality that Islam could be that bad. I thought it might be that the problem was with the people and not the religion.

However, on September 11, 2001, I saw the real face of Islam. I saw the happiness on the faces of our people because so many infidels were slaughtered so easily. I was shocked at the gloating of our people for killing innocent *kafirs.* I saw many people who started thanking Allah for this massacre. Our Islamic people said that Allah gave us our wish, and that this was the beginning of the destruction of *kafir* countries.

To me, this was sheer inhumanity.

Then, the *imam* implored Allah to help the Taliban against the U.S. military. I was angry. It was then that I stopped praying.

In 2004, I met my Pakistani manager, who, I believe, was anti-Islam. He made me feel like a human being again. He let me believe that I was, after all, not a crazy person. I stopped visiting the mosque, quit praying, and abandoned Ramadan fasting. Last Ramadan I did not observe a single fast.

Now I feel so happy and relieved. Without any guilt or fear, I now can watch movies and listen to music. I feel I am a human being and I am free to do whatever I like. I shall, from now on, tell the truth about this evil religion of Islam.

CHAPTER FIVE

FROM BELIEF TO ENLIGHTENMENT

"Allah was ignorant to the core. The Qur'an is full of errors...Allah could not have existed anywhere else except in the mind of a sick man. ...How disappointed I was when I realized all these years I had been praying to a fantasy."

WHILE IT IS EASY to call those who leave Islam "apostates," it is very difficult to be one.

"The process of going from faith to enlightenment is arduous and painful," and according to Ali Sina it is far from being an easy decision.

Born into a somewhat religious family, Ali became concerned about the fanatical teachings of the *mullahs* at his family's mosque. Furthermore, he could not understand the hatred many Muslims harbor against almost all non-Muslims. Ali also witnessed how the teachings he received about the Qur'an taught hatred and encouraged prejudice. Finding this hard to accept, he began to question how the Creator of the universe could be so cruel and myopic, especially in regarding women as imbeciles. In Islamic states the testimony of women is not admissible in court, and if a woman is raped she cannot accuse her rapist. Witnessing such abuses of women and their rights, Ali eventually began a Web site to reach out to other peaceful Muslims who might share his concerns. The Islamists quickly shut him down. However, he gathered enough strength to start again and today believes that the old way of killing apostates, burning their books, and silencing them can no longer work. In this modern age, Ali believes no one can stop people from reading and thinking critically, and that now the door of freedom of thought has been opened it can never be closed again.

Although Ali's site is banned in Saudi Arabia, the United Arab Emirates, and other Islamist countries, he believes that a great number of other Muslims who never knew the truth are being exposed for the first time and are shocked into reality. His testimony chronicles a long path to self-discovery. The tragedy on the pages of history is written with the blood of people killed in the name of God.

Ali's Testimony

I was born into a moderately religious family. On my mother's side I have a few relatives who are *ayatollahs*. Although my grandfather (whom I never met) was somewhat a skeptic, we were believers. My parents were not fond of the *mullahs*. In fact, we did not have much to do with our more fundamentalist relatives. We liked to think of ourselves as believing in "true Islam," not the one taught and practiced by the *mullahs*.

I recall discussing religion with the husband of one of my aunts when I was about fifteen years old. He was a fanatical Muslim who was very concerned about the *fiqh* (Islamic jurisprudence). It prescribes the way Muslims should pray, fast, run their public and private lives, do business, clean themselves, use the toilet, and even copulate. I argued this has nothing to do with true Islam, that it is a fabrication of the *mullahs*, that excessive attention to *fiqh* diminishes the impact and importance of the pure message of Islam—to unite man with his Creator. This view is mostly inspired by Sufism. Many Iranians, thanks to Rumi's poems, are to a great degree Sufis in their outlook.

In my early youth I noticed discriminations and cruelties against the members of religious minorities in Iran. This was more noticeable in provincial towns where the level of education was low and the *mullahs* had a better grip over gullible people. Due to my father's work we spent a few years in small towns out of the capital. I recall one of my teachers who planned to take the class swimming. We were excited and looked forward to it. In the class there were a couple of kids who were Baha'i and Jewish.

The teacher did not let them accompany us. He said they are not allowed to swim in the same pool that Muslims swim in. I cannot forget the kids' disappointment as they left school with tears in their eyes, subdued and heartbroken. At that age, maybe nine or ten, I could not make sense of and was saddened by this injustice. I thought it was the kids' fault for not being Muslims.

I believe I was lucky for having openminded parents who encouraged me to think critically. They tried to instill in me the love of God and his messenger, yet upheld humanistic values like equality of rights between man and woman, and love for all humankind. In a sense, this is how most modern Iranian families are. In fact, the majority of Muslims who have some education believe Islam is a humanistic religion that respects human rights, that elevates the status of women and protects their rights. Most Muslims believe that Islam means peace. Needless to say, few of them have read the Qur'an.

I spent my early youth in this sweet dream, advocating "true Islam" as I thought it should be, and criticizing the *mullahs* and their deviations from the real teachings of Islam. I idealized an Islam that conformed to my own humanistic values. Of course my imaginary Islam was a beautiful religion. It was a religion of equality and peace. It was a religion that encouraged its followers to go after knowledge and be inquisitive. It was a religion that was in harmony with science and reason. In fact, I thought that science got its inspiration from this religion. The Islam I believed was a religion that sparkled with modern science, which eventually bore its fruit in the West and made modern discoveries and inventions possible. Islam, I believed, was the real cause of modern civilization. The reason Muslims were living in such a miserable state of ignorance, I thought, was all the fault of the self-centered *mullahs* and religious leaders who for their own personal gain had misinterpreted the real teachings of Islam.

Many Muslims believe that the great Western civilization has its roots in Islam. They recall great Middle Eastern scientific minds whose contributions to science have been crucial in the birth of modern science. Omar Khayyam was a great mathematician who precisely calculated the length of the year to within .74 percent of a second. Zakaria Razi is regarded as one of the first founders of empirical science who based his knowledge on research and experimentation. Avicenna's (Bu Ali Sina) monumental encyclopedia of medicine was taught in European universities for centuries. There are so many more great luminaries who have "Islamic" names who were the pioneers of modern science when Europe was languishing in the medieval Dark Ages. Like all Muslims, I believed all these great men were Muslims, that they were inspired by the wealth of hidden knowledge in the Qur'an, and that if today's Muslims could regain the original purity of Islam, the long-lost glorious days of Islam would return and Muslims would lead the advancement of world civilization once again.

Iran was a Muslim country, but it was also a corrupt country. The chances of getting into a university were slim. Only one in ten applicants could get into the university. Often they were forced to choose subjects that they did not want to study because they could not get enough points for the subjects of their choice. Students with the right connections often got the seats.

The standard of education in Iran was not ideal. Universities were underfunded, as the Shah preferred building a powerful military to building the infrastructure of the country and investing in peoples' education. These were reasons why my father thought I would be better off to leave Iran to continue my education elsewhere.

We considered America and Europe, but my father, acting upon the counsel of a few of his religious friends, thought another Islamic country would be better for a sixteen-year-old boy. We were told that the West's morality is too lax, people are perverted, the beaches are full of nudes, and they drink and have licentious lifestyles, all of which are dangers to a young man. So I was sent to Pakistan instead, where people were religious and thus it was safe and moral. A friend of the family told us that Pakistan is just like England, except that it is cheaper.

This, of course, proved to be untrue. I found Pakistanis to be as immoral and corrupt as Iranians. Yes, they were very religious. They did not eat pork and I saw no one consuming alcohol in public, but I noticed that many had dirty minds, lied, were hypo-

crites, were cruel to women, and above all, were filled with hatred of the Indians. I did not find them better than Iranians in any
way. They were religious, but not moral or ethical.

In college, instead of taking Urdu I took Pakistani Culture to
complete my A level FSc (Fellow of Science). I learned the reason
for Pakistan's partition from India and for the first time heard
about Mohammad Ali Jinah, the man Pakistanis called Qaid-e
A'zam, the great leader. He was presented as an intelligent man,
the father of the nation, while Gandhi was spoken of in a derogatory way. Even then, I could not but side with Gandhi and condemn Jinah as an arrogant, ambitious man who was the culprit
for breaking up a country and causing millions of deaths. I always had a mind of my own and was a maverick in my thinking.
No matter what I was taught, I always came to my own conclusion and did not believe what I was told.

I did not see differences of religion as valid reasons for breaking up a country. The very word "Pakistan" was an insult to the
Indians. Pakistanis called themselves *pak* (clean) to distinguish
themselves from the Indians who were *najis* (unclean). Ironically,
I never saw a people dirtier than the Pakistanis, both physically
and mentally. It was disappointing to see another Islamic nation
in such intellectual and moral bankruptcy. In discussions with
my friends I failed to convince anyone of "true Islam." I condemned their bigotry and fanaticism while they disapproved of
me for my un-Islamic views.

I related all this to my father and decided to go to Italy for my
university studies. In Italy, people drink wine and eat pork, but
they were more hospitable, friendlier, and less hypocritical than
Muslims were. I noticed people were willing to help without expecting something in return. I met a very hospitable elderly couple, who invited me to have lunch with them on Sundays so I
would not have to stay home alone. They did not want anything
from me. They just wanted someone to love. I was almost a
grandson to them. Only strangers in a new country, who do not
know anyone and cannot speak the language, can truly appreciate the value of the help and hospitality of the locals.

Their house was sparkling clean, with shiny marble floors. This contradicted my idea of Westerners. Although my family was very open towards other people, Islam taught me that non-Muslims are *najies* (*Qur'an 9:28*) and one should not befriend them. I still have a copy of the Farsi translation of the Qur'an I used to often read from. One of the underlined verses is:

> O you who believe! Take not the Jews and the Christians as *awliya'* (friends, protectors, helpers, etc.), they are but be *awliya'* to one another. *Qur'an 5: 51*

I had difficulty understanding the wisdom of such a verse. I wondered why I should not befriend this wonderful elderly couple who had no ulterior motives in showing me their hospitality other than just making me feel at home. I thought they were "true Muslims" and I tried to raise the subject of religion, hoping they would see the truth of Islam and embrace it. But they were not interested and politely changed the subject. I was not stupid enough at any time in my life to believe that all nonbelievers would go to hell. I read this in the Qur'an before but never wanted to think about it. I simply brushed it off or ignored it. Of course, I knew that God would be pleased if someone recognized his messenger but never thought he would actually be cruel enough to burn someone in hell for eternity, even if that person only does good deeds, just because he was not a Muslim. I read the following warning:

> If anyone desires a religion other than Islam (submission to Allah), never will it be accepted of him; and in the Hereafter He will be in the ranks of those who have lost (all spiritual good). *Qur'an 3:85*

Yet I paid little heed and tried to convince myself the meaning is something other than what it appears to be. At that moment this was not a subject that I was ready to handle. So I did not think about it.

I hung around with my Muslim friends and noticed that most of them lived a very immoral life of double standards. Most of them found girlfriends and slept with them. That was very un-Islamic, or so I thought at that time. What bothered me most was they did not value these girls as real human beings who deserved respect. These girls were not Muslim girls and therefore were used just for sex. This attitude was not general. Those who made less show of religiosity were more respectful and sincere towards their Western girlfriends and some even loved them and wanted to marry them. Paradoxically, those who were more religious were less faithful towards their girlfriends. I always thought that true Islam is what is right. If something is immoral, unethical, dishonest, or cruel, it cannot be Islam. I could not see how the behavior of these immoral and callous Muslims could be the result of what was taught in Islam.

Years later, I realized that the truth is exactly the opposite. I found many verses that were disturbing and made me revise my whole opinion of Islam. As I saw it, the tragedy was that the very same people who lived unethically and immorally were the ones who called themselves Muslims, said their prayers, fasted, and were the first to defend Islam angrily if anyone raised a question about it. They were the ones who would lose their tempers and start a fight if someone dared to say a word against Islam.

Once I befriended a young Iranian man at the university restaurant, later introducing him to two other Muslim friends of mine. We were all about the same age. He was an erudite, virtuous, wise young man. My other two friends and I were captivated by his charm and high moral values. We used to wait for him and sit next to him during lunch hour, as we always learned something from him. We used to eat a lot of spaghetti and risotto and craved a good Persian *ghorme sabzi* and *chelow*. Our friend said his mother sent him some dried vegetables and invited us to his house the next Sunday for lunch. We found his two-room apartment very clean, unlike the houses of other guys. He made us a delicious *ghorme sabzi*, which we ate with great gusto, and then we sat back chatting and sipping our tea. It was then we noticed his Baha'i books. When we asked about them, he said he was a Baha'i.

That did not bother me at all, but on the way home my two friends said they did not wish to continue their friendship with him. I was surprised and asked why. They said that being a Baha'i makes him *najis* and had they known he was a Baha'i, they would not have befriended him. I was puzzled and inquired why they thought he was *najis* if we all were complementing him on his cleanliness. We all agreed he was a morally superior man to all of the Muslim young men we knew, so why this sudden change of attitude? Their response was very disturbing. They said the name itself had something in it that made them dislike this religion. They asked me if I knew why everyone disliked the Baha'is. I told them I didn't know, and that I liked everyone. But since they disliked the Baha'is, perhaps they should explain their reasons. They did not know why! This man was the first Baha'i they knew this well, and he was an exemplary man. I wanted to know the reason for their dislike. There was no particular reason, they said. It's just they knew that Baha'is are bad.

I am happy I did not continue my friendship with these two bigots. From them I learned how prejudice is formed and operates.

Later I realized the prejudices and hatred that Muslims harbor against almost all non-Muslims are not the result of any misinterpretation of the teachings of the Qur'an, but is because this book teaches hate and encourages prejudice. Those Muslims who go to the mosques and listen to the sermons of the *mullahs* are affected. There are many verses in the Qur'an that call believers to hate nonbelievers, fight them, call them *najis*, subdue and humiliate them, chop off their heads and limbs, crucify them, and kill them wherever they find them.

I left religion on the back burner for several years. Not that my views about religion had changed or I didn't consider myself religious anymore. I just had so much to do that expending time on religion had become difficult. Meanwhile, I learned more about democracy, human rights, and other values, like equality of rights between men and women, and I liked what I learned. Did I pray? Whenever I could, but not fanatically. After all, I was living and working in a Western country and did not want to look too different.

One day, I decided that it was time to deepen my knowledge of Islam and read the Qur'an from cover to cover. I found an Arabic copy of the Qur'an with an English translation. Previously I read only bits and pieces of the Qur'an. This time I read all of it.

I would read a verse in Arabic, then its English translation, then refer back to the Arabic, and did not read the next verse until I was completely satisfied I understood the Arabic.

It didn't take long before I came upon verses I found hard to accept. One of these verses was:

> Allah forgiveth not that partners should be set up with Him; but He forgiveth anything else, to whom He pleaseth; to set up partners with Allah is to devise a sin Most heinous indeed. *Qur'an 4:48*

I found it hard to accept that Gandhi would burn in hell forever because he was a polytheist with no hope of redemption, while a Muslim murderer could hope to receive Allah's forgiveness. This raised a disturbing question: *Why is Allah so desperate to be known as the only God? If there is no other god but him, what is the fuss? Against whom is he competing? Why should he even care whether anyone knows him and praises him or not?*

Now that I had lived in the West and had many Western friends who were kind to me, liked me, opened their hearts and homes to me, and accepted me as their friend, it was really hard to accept that Allah didn't want me to befriend them.

> Let not the believers take for friends or helpers unbelievers rather than believers: if any do that, in nothing will there be help from Allah. *Qur'an 3:28*

Isn't Allah the Creator of the unbelievers, too? Isn't he the God of everybody? Why should he be so unkind to the unbelievers? Wouldn't it be better if Muslims befriended unbelievers and taught them Islam by a good example? By keeping ourselves aloof and distant from unbelievers, the gap of misunderstandings will never be bridged. How in the world will unbelievers learn about Islam if we do not associate with them? These were the questions I kept asking myself. The answer to these questions came in a very disconcerting verse. Allah's order was to, "slay them wherever ye catch them" (*Qur'an 2:191*).

I thought of my own friends, remembering their kindnesses and love for me, and wondered how in the world a true God would ask anyone to kill another human being just because he does not believe. That seemed absurd, yet this concept was repeated so often in the Qur'an there was no doubt about it. In verse 8:65, Allah tells his Prophet:

> O Prophet! Rouse the believers to the fight. If there are twenty amongst you, patient and persevering, they will vanquish two hundred: if a hundred, they will vanquish a thousand of the unbelievers.

I wondered why Allah would send a messenger to make war. *Shouldn't God teach us to love each other and be tolerant toward each other's beliefs? And if Allah is really so concerned about making people believe in him to the extent that he would kill them if they don't believe, why would he not kill them himself? Why does he ask us to do his dirty work? Are we Allah's hit men?*

Although I knew of *jihad* and never questioned it before, I found it hard to accept that God would resort to imposing such violent measures on people. What was more shocking was the cruelty of Allah in dealing with unbelievers.

> I will instill terror into the hearts of the unbelievers: smite ye above their necks and smite all their fingertips off them. *Qur'an 8:12*

It seemed Allah was not just satisfied with killing unbelievers; he enjoyed torturing them before killing them. Smiting people's heads from above their necks and chopping their fingertips were very cruel acts. Would God really give such orders? And yet the worst is what he promised to do with unbelievers in the other world.

How could the Creator of this universe be so cruel? I was shocked to learn that the Qur'an tells Muslims to: kill unbelievers wherever they find them (*Qur'an 2:191*), murder them and treat them harshly (*Qur'an 9:123*), fight them (*Qur'an 8:65*) until no other religion than Islam is left (*Qur'an 2:193*), humiliate them and impose on them a penalty tax if they are Christians or Jews (*Qur'an 9:29*), slay them if they are pagans (*Qur'an 9:5*), crucify, or cut off their hands and feet, and expel them from the land in disgrace. And as if this were not enough, Muslims are told that unbelievers "shall have a great punishment in world hereafter" (*Qur'an 5:34*), not to befriend their own fathers or brothers if they are not believers (*Qur'an 3:28, 9:23*), to kill their own family in the battles of Badr and Uhud, and to "strive against the unbelievers with great endeavor" (*Qur'an 25:52*) and be stern with them because they belong to hell (*Qur'an 66:9*).

How can any sensible person remain unmoved when he or she finds the Qur'an saying: "strike off the heads of the unbelievers" then after a "wide slaughter among them, carefully tie up the remaining captives" (*Qur'an 47:4*)?

I was also shocked to learn the Qur'an denies freedom of belief for all and clearly states Islam is the only acceptable religion (*Qur'an 3:85*). Allah relegates those who do not believe in the Qur'an to hell (*Qur'an 5:11*) and calls them *najis* (filthy, untouchable, impure) (*Qur'an 9:28*). He says unbelievers will go to hell and will drink boiling water (*Qur'an 14:17*). Further, "As for the unbelievers, for them garments of fire shall be cut and there shall be poured over their heads boiling water whereby whatever is in their bowls and skin shall be dissolved and they will be punished with hooked iron rods" (*Qur'an 22:9*). How sadistic!

The book of Allah says women are inferior to men and their husbands have the right to beat them (*Qur'an 4:34*), and that women will go to hell if they are disobedient to their husbands (*Qur'an 66:10*). It says men have an advantage over women (*Qur'an 2:228*). It not only denies women equal rights to their inheritance (*Qur'an 4:11-12*), it also regards them as imbeciles and decrees that their testimony alone is not admissible in court (*Qur'an 2:282*). This means that a woman who is raped cannot accuse her rapist unless she can produce a male witness, which of course is a joke. Rapists don't rape in the presence of witnesses. But the most shocking verse is where Allah allows Muslims to rape women captured in wars even if they are married before being captured (*Qur'an 4:3, 24*). The holy Prophet raped the prettiest women he captured in his raids on the same day he killed their husbands and loved ones. This is why anytime a Muslim army subdues another nation, they call them *kafir* and rape their women.

Pakistani soldiers raped up to 250,000 Bengali women in 1971 and massacred three million unarmed civilians when their religious leader decreed that Bangladeshis are un-Islamic. This is why the prison guards in the Islamic regime of Iran rape the women and then kill them after calling them apostates and the enemies of Allah.

The Qur'an is full of verses that teach killing of unbelievers and how Allah will torture them after they die. There are no lessons on morality, justice, honesty, or love. The only message of the Qur'an is to believe in Allah and his messenger. The Qur'an coaxes people with celestial rewards of unlimited sex in paradise and threatens them with blazing fires of hell. When the Qur'an speaks of righteousness, it does not mean righteousness as we understand it, but it means belief in Allah and his messenger. A Muslim can be a killer and murder non-Muslims and yet be a righteous person. Good actions are secondary. Belief in Allah and his messenger are the ultimate purpose of a person's life.

After reading the Qur'an I became greatly depressed. It was hard to accept it all. At first I denied and searched for esoteric meanings to these cruel verses of the Qur'an, all in vain. There was no misunderstanding! The Qur'an was overwhelmingly inhumane. Of course it contained a lot of scientific heresies and absurdities, but they were not what impacted me the most. It was the violence of this book that really jolted me and shook the foundation of my belief.

After my bitter experience with the Qur'an I found myself traveling on a torturous road riddled with torments. I was kicked out of the blissful garden of ignorance, where all my questions were answered. There I did not have to think. All I had to do was believe. Now, the gates to that garden were closed to me forever. I had committed the unthinkable sin of thinking. I had eaten from the forbidden tree of knowledge, and my eyes had been opened. I could see the fallacy of it all and my own nakedness. I knew I would not be let into that paradise of oblivion again. Once you start thinking, you don't belong there anymore. I had only one way to go: forward.

This road to enlightenment proved to be more arduous than I was prepared for. It was slippery. There were mountains of obstacles to climb and precipices of errors to avert. I traveled uncharted territories alone, not knowing what I would find next. It would become my odyssey in the realm of understanding and discovering truth, eventually leading me to the land of enlightenment and freedom.

I will chart these territories for all those who also commit the sin of thinking, find themselves kicked out of the paradise of ignorance, and are en route to an unknown destination.

If you doubt, if the mantle of ignorance in which you wrapped yourself is shredded to pieces and you find yourself naked, know that you cannot stay in the paradise of ignorance any longer. You have been cast out forever. Just as a child once out of the womb cannot go back, you will not be readmitted into that blissful garden of oblivion again. Listen to one who has been there and done that, and don't cling despondently to the gates. That door is locked.

Instead look forward. You have a trip ahead of you. You can fly to your destination or you can crawl. I crawled! But because I crawled, I know this path quite well. I will chart the road, so hopefully you don't have to crawl.

The passage from faith to enlightenment consists of seven valleys.

The first valley is shock. After reading the Qur'an my perspective was jolted. I found myself standing face-to-face with the truth and I was scared to look at it. It certainly was not what I was expecting to see. I had no one to blame, to curse and call a liar. I found the absurdity of Islam and inhumanity of its author by reading the Qur'an. And I was shocked. Only this shock made me come to my senses and face the truth. Unfortunately, this is a very difficult, painful process. The followers of Mohammad must see the naked truth and they must be shocked. We cannot keep sugarcoating the truth. The truth is bitter and it must be accepted. Facts are stubborn and refuse to go away. Only then does the process of enlightenment start.

But because each person's sensitivity is different, what shocks one person may not shock the other. Even as a man I was shocked when I read that Mohammad instructed his followers to beat their wives and called women "deficient in intelligence." Yet I have come to know many Muslim women who have no difficulty accepting these derogatory statements uttered by their

Prophet. It's not that they agree they are deficient in intelligence or they believe the majority of the inhabitants of hell are women just because the Prophet said so, but they simply block out that information. They read it, but it doesn't sink in. They are in denial. The denial acts as a shield that covers and protects them, that saves them from facing the pain of reality. Once that shield is up, nothing can bring it down. At this point their beliefs must be attacked from other directions. We have to bombard them with other shocking teachings of the Qur'an. They may have a weak spot for one of them. That is all they need: a good shock. Shocks are painful, but they can be lifesavers. Shocks are used by doctors to bring back to life a dead patient.

For the first time, the Internet has changed the balance of power. Now the brutal force of the guns, prisons, and death squads is helpless and the pen is almighty. For the first time, Muslims cannot stop the truth by killing its messenger. Now a great number of them are coming in contact with the truth and they feel helpless. They want to silence this voice, but they cannot. They want to kill the messenger, but they cannot. They try to ban the sites exposing their cherished beliefs; sometimes they succeed momentarily, but most of the time they don't. I created a site to educate Muslims about true Islam. I hosted it at Tripod.com. The Islamists forced Tripod to shut it down and the cowardly Tripod executives complied to appease those Muslims. I got my domain and the site was back again in a couple of weeks. Therefore, the old way of killing the apostates, burning their books, and silencing them by terror does not work. They cannot stop people from reading. Even though my site is banned in Saudi Arabia, Emirates, and many other Islamic countries, a great number of Muslims who never knew the truth about Islam are being exposed to the truth for the first time, and are shocked.

I met a lady on the Internet who converted to Islam and started to wear the Islamic veil. She had a Web site with her picture completely covered in a black veil along with her story of how she became a Muslim. She was very active and she used to advise others not to read my writings. However, when she read the story of Safiyah, the Jewish woman that Mohammad captured and raped after killing her father, husband, and many of her relatives, she was shocked. She questioned other Muslims about this in vain. Then the door was open and she was cast out of the paradise of ignorance. She kept writing to me and asking questions. Finally, she passed through the other stages from blind faith to enlightenment very quickly and wrote thanking me for guiding her through this arduous path. She withdrew from the Yahoo! Islamic clubs altogether.

When people learn about the unholy life of Mohammad and the absurdities of the Qur'an, they are shocked. I want to expose Islam; write the truth about Mohammad's unholy life, his hateful words, his senseless assertions; and bombard Muslims with facts. They will be angry. They will curse me, insult me, and tell me that after reading my articles their faith in Islam is "strengthened." But that is when I know that I have sown the seed of doubt in their mind. They say all this because they are shocked and have entered the stage of denial. The seed of doubt is planted and it will germinate. In some people it takes years, but given the chance it will eventually bloom.

Doubt is the greatest gift we can give to each other. It is the gift of enlightenment. Doubt will set us free, will advance knowledge, and will unravel the mysteries of this universe.

One of the hurdles to overcome is the tradition and false values imposed on us by thousands of years of religious upbringing. The world still values faith and considers doubt a sign of weakness. People talk of men of faith with respect and disdain men of little faith. We are screwed up in our values.

Doubt, on the other hand, means the reverse of the above. It means being capable of thinking independently, of questioning, and of being a skeptic. We owe our science and our modern civilization to men and women who doubted—not to those who believed. Those who doubted were the pioneers; they were the leaders of thought. They were philosophers, inventors, and discoverers. Those who believed lived and died as followers, and made little or no contribution to the advancement of science and human understanding.

After being shocked, or maybe simultaneously, one denies. The majority of Muslims are trapped in denial. They are unable and unwilling to admit the Qur'an is a hoax. They desperately try to explain the unexplainable, find miracles in it, and would willingly bend all the rules of logic to prove that the Qur'an is right. Each time they are exposed to a shocking statement in the Qur'an or a reprehensible act performed by Mohammad, they retreat in denial. This is what I did in the first phase of my journey. Denial is a safe place. It is the unwillingness to admit that you have been kicked out of the paradise of ignorance. You try to go back, reluctant to take the next step forward. In denial you find your comfort zone. In denial you are not going to be hurt, everything is okay; everything is fine.

Truth is extremely painful, especially if one has been accustomed to lies all his life. It is not easy for a Muslim to see Mohammad for who he was. It is like telling a child that his father is a murderer, a rapist, and a thief. A child who adulates his father will not be able to accept it even if all the proofs in the world are shown to him. The shock is so great that all he can do is deny it. He will call you a liar, hate you for hurting him, curse you, consider you his enemy, and may even explode in anger and physically attack you.

This is the stage of denial. It is a self-defense mechanism. If pain is too great, denial will take that pain away. If a mother is informed that her child has died in an accident, her first reaction is often denial. At the moment of great catastrophes, one is usually overwhelmed by a weary sense that this is all a bad dream and that eventually you'll wake up and everything will be okay. Unfortunately, facts are stubborn and will not go away. One can live in denial for a while, but sooner or later the truth must be accepted.

Muslims are cocooned in lies. Because speaking against Islam is a crime punishable by death, no one dares to tell the truth. Those who do, do not live long. They are quickly silenced. So how would you know the truth if all you hear are lies? On one hand the Qur'an claims to be a miracle and challenges anyone to produce a *Surah* like it:

> And if you are in doubt as to which we have revealed to our
> servant, then produce a *Surah* like it, and call on your helper,
> besides Allah, if you are truthful. *Qur'an 2:23*

Then it instructs its followers to kill anyone who dares to criticize
it or challenge it. If you ever dare to take up the challenge and
produce a *Surah* as poorly written as the Qur'an, you will be accused of mocking Islam, for which the punishment is death. In
this atmosphere of insincerity and deceit, truth is the casualty.

The pain of coming face-to-face with the truth and realizing
all that we believed were lies is extremely agonizing. The only
mechanism and natural way to deal with it is denial. Denial takes
away the pain. It is a soothing bliss, even though it is hiding one's
head in the sand.

One cannot stay in denial forever. Soon the night will fall and
the cold shivering reality freezes one's bones, and you realize that
you are out of the paradise of ignorance. That door is closed and
the key has been thrown away. You know too much. You are an
outcast. Fearfully you look at the dark and twining road barely
visible in the twilight of your uncertainties, and gingerly you take
your first steps towards an unknown destiny. You grapple and
fumble, reluctantly trying to stay focused. But fear overwhelms
you and each time you try to run back to the garden you once
again face the closed door.

The great majority of Muslims live in denial. They stay behind the closed door. They cannot go back nor do they dare to
walk away from it. Those who are inside the garden are those
who never left it. This door will only let you out. You cannot get
in. That blissful garden is the garden of certitude. It is reserved
for the faithful, for those who do not doubt, for those who do not
think. They believe anything. They would believe that night is
day and day is night. They would believe that Mohammad
climbed to the seventh heaven, met with God, split the moon,
and conversed with *jinns*.

These believers will never see the truth if they are permanently
kept cocooned in lies. All they have heard so far is the lie that Islam
is good and if only Muslims practiced true Islam, the world would
become a paradise; that the problems of Islam are all the fault of

Muslims. This is a lie. Most Muslims are good people. They are no worse and no better than others. It's Islam that makes them commit atrocities. Those Muslims who do bad things are those who follow Islam. Islam rears the criminal instinct in people. The more a person is Islamist, the more bloodthirsty, hate mongering, and the more of a zombie she or he becomes.

I wanted to deny what I was reading. I wanted to believe that the real meaning of the Qur'an is something else, but I could not. I could no longer fool myself by saying these inhumane verses were taken out of context. The Qur'an does not have a context. Verses are jammed together at random, often lacking any coherence.

Those who read my articles and are hurt by what I say about the Qur'an and Islam are lucky. They have me to blame. They can hate me, curse me, and direct all their anger at me. However, when I read the Qur'an and learned about its content, I could not blame anyone. After going through the stages of shock and denial, I was confused and blamed myself. I hated myself for thinking, for doubting and for finding fault with what I regarded to be the words of God.

Like all other Muslims, I was exposed to and accepted all the many lies, absurdities, and inhumanities. I was brought up as a religious person. I believed in whatever I was told. These lies were given to me in small doses, gradually, since my childhood. I was never given an alternative to compare. It is like vaccination. I was immune to the truth. But when I started to read the Qur'an seriously from cover to cover and understood what this book is saying, I felt nauseated. All those lies suddenly appeared in front of me.

I had heard them all and had accepted them. My rational thinking was numbed. I had become insensitive to the absurdities of the Qur'an. When I found something that did not make sense, I brushed it off and said to myself that one has to look at the "big picture." That idyllic big picture, however, was nowhere to be found except in my own mind. I pictured a perfect Islam; so all those absurdities did not bother me because I paid no attention to them. When I read the whole Qur'an, I discovered a distinctly different picture than the one in my mind. The new picture of

Islam emerging from the pages of the Qur'an was violent, intolerant, irrational, arrogant; a far cry from Islam as a religion of peace, equality, and tolerance.

In the face of this much absurdity, I had to deny it to keep my sanity. Nevertheless, how long could I keep denying the truth when it was out like the sun right in front of me? I was reading the Qur'an in Arabic so I could not blame a bad translation. Later I read other translations. I realized many translations in English are not entirely reliable. The translators had tried very hard to hide the inhumanity and the violence in the Qur'an by twisting the words and adding their own words sometimes in parenthesis or brackets to soften its harsh tone. The Arabic Qur'an is more shocking than its English translations.

I was confused and I did not know where to turn. My faith had been shaken and my world had crumbled. I could no longer deny what I was reading. However, I could not accept the possibility that this was all a huge lie. *How could it be,* I kept asking myself, *that so many people have not seen the truth and I could see it? How could great seers like Jalaleddin Rumi not see that Mohammad was an impostor and that the Qur'an is a hoax, and I see it?* It was then that I entered the stage of guilt.

The guilt lasted for many months. I hated myself for having these thoughts. I felt God was testing my faith. I felt ashamed. I spoke with learned people whom I trusted, people who were not only knowledgeable but whom I thought were wise. I heard very little that could quench the burning fire within me. One of these learned men told me not to read the Qur'an for a while. He told me to pray and read only books that would strengthen my faith. I did that, but it did not help. The thoughts about the absurd, sometimes ruthless, ridiculous verses of the Qur'an kept throbbing in my head. Each time I looked at my bookshelf and saw that book, I felt pain. I took it and hid it behind the other books. I thought if I did not think about it for a while, my negative thoughts would go away and I would regain my faith once again. They didn't go away. I denied as much as I could, until I could no longer. I was shocked, confused, felt guilty, and it was painful.

This period of guilt lasted too long. One day I decided enough is enough. I told myself that it is not my fault. *I am not going to carry this guilt forever, thinking about things that make no sense to me. If God gave me a brain, it is because he wants me to use it. If what I perceive as right and wrong is skewed, then it is not my fault.*

He tells me killing is bad and I know it is bad because I do not want to be killed. Then why did his messenger kill so many innocent people and order his followers to kill those who do not believe? If rape is bad, and I know it is bad because I do not want it to happen to people I love, why did Allah's Prophet rape the women he captured in war? If slavery is bad, and I know it is bad because I hate to lose my freedom and become a slave, why has the Prophet of God enslaved so many people and made himself rich by selling them? If imposition of religion is bad, and I know that it is bad because I do not like another person to force on me a religion that I don't want, then why did the Prophet eulogize jihad *and exhort his followers to kill unbelievers, take their booty, and distribute their women and children as spoils of war? If God tells me something is good, and I know that it is good because it feels good to me, then why did his Prophet do the opposite of that thing?*

When this guilt was lifted off my shoulders, dismay, disillusionment, or cynicism followed. I felt sorry for having wasted so many years of my life, and for all the Muslims who are still trapped in these foolish beliefs, for all those who lost their lives in the name of these false doctrines, for all the women in virtually all the Islamic countries who suffer all sorts of abuses and oppressions. They do not even know they are being abused.

I thought of all the wars waged in the name of religion—so many people died for nothing. Millions of believers left their homes and families to wage war in the name of God, never to return, thinking they are spreading faith in God. They massacred millions of innocent people. Civilizations destroyed, libraries burned, and so much knowledge lost—for nothing. I recalled my father waking up in the early hours of the morning and in the icy water of the winter performing voodoo. I recalled him coming home hungry and thirsty during the month of fasting, and I thought of the billions of people who torture themselves in this way for nothing. The realization that all that I believed was a lie and all that I did was a waste of my life, and the fact that a billion other people are still lost in this arid desert of ignorance chasing a mirage that to them appears to be water was disappointing.

Prior to that God was always in the back of my mind. I used to talk to him in my imagination and those conversations seemed real to me. I thought God was watching and taking account of every good act that I did. The feeling that someone was watching over me, guiding my steps, and protecting me was very comforting. It was difficult to accept that there is no such thing as Allah and even if there is a God, it is not Allah. I did not give up the belief in God, but by then I knew for sure that if this universe has a maker, it couldn't be the deity that Mohammad had envisioned. Allah was ignorant to the core. The Qur'an is full of errors. No Creator of this universe could be as stupid as the god of the Qur'an appeared to be. Allah could not have existed anywhere else except in the mind of a sick man. I understood that he was but a figment of Mohammad's imagination and nothing more. How disappointed I was when I realized all these years I had been praying to a fantasy.

This feeling of loss and disappointment was accompanied by a sense of sadness, or some kind of depression. It was as if my whole world had fallen apart. I felt like the ground I was standing on was no longer there and I was falling into a bottomless pit. Without exaggerating, it felt like I was in hell.

I was bewildered, pleading for help, and no one could. I felt ashamed of my thoughts and hated myself for having such thoughts. The guilt was accompanied by a profound sense of loss and depression. As a rule, I am a positive thinker. I see the good side of everything. I always think tomorrow is going to be better than today. I am not the kind of person who is easily depressed. However, this feeling of loss was overwhelming. I still recall that weight in my heart. I thought God has forsaken me and I did not know why. *"Is that God's punishment?"* I kept asking myself. I do not remember hurting anyone ever. I went out of my way to help anyone whose life crossed mine and asked me for help. *So, why does God want to punish me in this way? Why is he not answering my prayers? Why has he left me to myself and these thoughts I can find no answers to? Does he want to test me? Then where are the answers to my prayers? Will I pass this test if I become stupid and stop using my brain? If so, why did he give me a brain? Would only dumb people pass the test of faith?*

I felt betrayed and violated. I cannot say which feeling was predominant. At times I was disillusioned, sad, or dismayed. Even if faith is false, it is still sweet. It is very comforting to believe.

Juxtaposing my feelings of sadness and loss, I felt liberated. Curiously I no longer felt confused or guilty. I knew for sure the Qur'an was a hoax and Mohammad was an impostor.

To overcome this sadness I tried to keep myself busy with other activities. I even took dancing lessons and experienced what it means to be alive, to be free of guilt, to enjoy life and to be normal. I realized how much I had missed and how foolishly I deprived myself of the simple pleasures of life. Of course, denial is how cults exert their control over their believers. I denied myself the simplest pleasures of life, was living in constant fear of God, and I thought this was normal. I am talking of pleasures like sleeping in in the morning, dancing, dating, or sipping a glass of fine wine.

At this time, I entered another stage of my spiritual journey to enlightenment. I became angry. Angry for having believed those lies for so many years, for wasting so many years of my life chasing a wild goose. Angry at my culture for betraying me, for the wrong values it gave me; with my parents for teaching me a lie; with myself for not thinking before, for believing in lies, trusting an impostor; with God for letting me down, for not intervening and stopping the lies that were being disseminated in his name.

When I saw pictures of millions of Muslims who, with so much devotion, went to Saudi Arabia, many of them spending their life's savings to perform *hajj*, I became angry at the lies these people were brought up with. When I read someone had converted to Islam, something Muslims love to advertise and make a big issue of, I became saddened and angry. I was sad for that poor soul and angry with the lies.

I was angry at the whole world that tries to protect this lie, that defends it and even abuses you if you raise your voice to try to tell them what you know. It is not just Muslims, but even Westerners who do not believe in Islam. It's okay to criticize anything but Islam. What amazed me and made me even angrier was the resistance I faced when I tried to tell others that Islam is not the truth.

Fortunately, this anger did not last long. I knew that Mohammad was no messenger of God but a charlatan, a demagogue whose only intention was to beguile people and satisfy his own narcissistic ambitions. I knew all those childish stories of a hell with scorching fire and a heaven with rivers of wine, milk, and honey were the figments of a sick, wild, insecure, and bullying mind of a man in desperate need to dominate and affirm his own authority.

I realized I could not be angry with my parents; for they did their best and taught me what they thought to be the best. I could not be angry at my society or culture because my people were just as misinformed as my parents and myself. After some thought, I realized everyone was a victim. There are one billion or more victims. Even those who have become victimizers are victims of Islam, too. How could I blame Muslims if they do not know what Islam stands for and honestly, though erroneously, believe that it is a religion of peace?

What about Mohammad? Should I be angry with him for lying, deceiving, and misleading people? How could I be angry with a dead person? Mohammad was an emotionally sick man who was not in control of himself. He grew up as an orphan in the care of five different foster parents before he reached the age of eight. As soon as he became attached to someone, he was snatched away and given to someone else. This must have been hard on him and was detrimental to his emotional health. As a child, deprived of love and a sense of belonging, he grew with deep feelings of fear and lack of self-confidence. He became a narcissist. A narcissist is a person who has not received enough love in his childhood, who is incapable of loving, but instead craves attention, respect, and recognition. He sees his own worth in the way others view him. Without that recognition he is nobody. He becomes a manipulater and a pathetic liar.

Narcissists are grandiose dreamers. They want to conquer the world and dominate everyone. Only in their megalomaniac reveries is their narcissism satisfied. Some famous narcissists are Hitler, Mussolini, Stalin, Saddam Hussein, Idi Amin, Pol Pot, and Mao. Narcissists are intelligent, yet emotional wrecks. They are deeply disturbed people. They set themselves extremely high goals. Their goals always have to do with domination, power, and respect. They are nobody if they are neglected. Narcissists often seek justification to impose their control over their unwary victims. For Hitler it was the party and race. For Mussolini it was fascism or the unity of the nation against others. For Mohammad it was religion.

These causes are just tools in their quest for power. Instead of promoting themselves, the narcissists promote a cause, an ideology, or a religion while presenting themselves as the only authority and the representative of these causes. Hitler did not call the Germans to love him as a person but to love and respect him because he was the *Führer*. Mohammad could not ask anyone to obey him. However, he could easily demand his followers obey Allah and his messenger. Of course, Allah was Mohammad's own alter ego, so all the obedience was to him in the final account. In this way Mohammad could wield control over everyone's life by telling him or her he is the representative of God and what he says is what God has ordained.

Mohammad was a ruthless man with no feelings. When he decided the Jews were of no use to him, he stopped kowtowing to them and eliminated them all. He massacred all the men of Bani Qurayza and banished or murdered every other Jew and Christian from Arabia. Surely if God wanted to destroy these people he would not have needed the help of his messenger.

Therefore, I found there was no reason to be angry with an emotionally sick man who died a long time ago. Mohammad was a victim himself of the stupid culture of his people, of the ignorance of his mother who, instead of keeping him during the first years of his life when he needed her love most, entrusted him to a Bedouin woman to raise him so she could find a new husband.

I could not criticize or blame the ignorant Arabs of the seventh century for not being able to discern that Mohammad was sick and not a prophet, that his outlandish promises, his impressive dreams of conquering and subduing the great nations when he was just a pauper, were caused by his pathological emotional complications and were not due to a divine power. How could I blame those ignorant Arabs for falling prey to a man like Mohammad when only in the last century, millions of Germans fell prey to the charisma of another narcissist who, just as Mohammad, made big promises and was as ruthless, as manipulative, and as ambitious as he was?

After serious thought, I realized there is not a single person I could be angry with. I realized we are all victims and victimizers at the same time. The culprit is ignorance. Because of our ignorance we believe in charlatans and their lies, allowing them to disseminate hate among us in the name of false deities, ideologies, or religions. This hate separates us from each other, and prevents us from seeing our oneness and understanding that we are all members of the human race, related to each other and interdependent.

It was then that my anger gave way to a profound feeling of empathy, compassion, and love. I made a promise to myself to fight this ignorance that divides the human race. We paid, and are paying, dearly for our disunity. This disunity is caused by ignorance and the ignorance is the result of false beliefs and pernicious ideologies that are concocted by emotionally unhealthy individuals for self-serving purposes.

Ideologies separate us. Religions cause disunity, hate, fighting, killing, and antagonism. As members of the human race, we need no ideology, cause, or religion to be united.

I realized that the purpose of life is not to believe, but to doubt. I realized that no one can teach us the truth because truth cannot be taught. It can only be experienced. No religion, philosophy, or doctrine can teach you the truth. Truth is in the love we have for our fellow human beings, in the laughter of a child, in friendship, in companionship, in the love of a parent and a child, and in our relationships with others. Truth is not in ideologies. The only thing that is real is love.

The process of going from faith to enlightenment is an arduous and painful process. Let us borrow a term from Sufism and call that the seven "valleys" of enlightenment.

Faith is the state of being confirmed in ignorance. You will continue to stay in that state of blissful ignorance until you are shocked and forced out of it. This shock is the first valley.

The natural first reaction to shock is denial. Denial acts like a shield. It buffers the pain and protects you from the agony of going out of your comfort zone. The comfort zone is where we feel at ease, where we find everything familiar, where we don't face new challenges or the unknown. This is the second valley.

Growth doesn't take place in comfort zones. In order to go forward and evolve we need to get out of our comfort zones. We won't do that unless we are shocked. It is also natural to buffer the pain of shock by denial. At this moment we need another shock, and we may decide to shield ourselves again with another denial. The more a person is exposed to facts and the more he is shocked, the more he tries to protect himself with more denials. However, denials do not eliminate the facts. They just shield us momentarily. When we are exposed to facts, at a certain point we will be unable to continue denying. Suddenly we won't be able to keep our defenses up and the wall of denials will come down. We can't keep hiding our heads in the sand perpetually. Once doubt sets in, it will have a domino effect and we find ourselves hit from all directions by facts that up until now we avoided and denied. Suddenly all those absurdities that we accepted and even defended are no longer logical and we reject them.

We are then driven into the painful stage of confusion and that is the third valley. The old beliefs seem unreasonable, foolish, and unacceptable, yet we have nothing to cling to. This valley, I believe, is the most dreadful stage in the passage from faith to enlightenment. In this valley we lose our faith without having found the enlightenment. We are standing in nowhere. We experience a free fall. We ask for help but all we get is a rehashing of some nonsensical clichés. It seems that those who try to help us are lost themselves, yet they are so convinced. They believe in what they don't know. The arguments they present are not logical at all. They expect us to believe without questioning. They bring the example of the faith of others. But the intensity of the faith of other people does not prove the truth of what they believe in.

This confusion eventually gives way to the fourth valley, guilt. You feel guilty for thinking. You feel guilty for doubting, for questioning, for not understanding. You feel naked, and ashamed of your thoughts. You think it is your fault if the absurdities mentioned in your holy books make no sense to you. You think that God has abandoned you or that he is testing your faith. In this valley you are torn apart by your emotions and your intellect. Emotions are not rational, but they are extremely powerful. You want to go back to the paradise of ignorance; you desperately want to believe, but you simply can't. You have committed the sin of thinking. You have eaten the forbidden fruit from the tree of knowledge. You have angered the god of your imaginations.

Finally you decide there is no need to feel guilty for the understanding. That guilt does not belong to you. You feel liberated but at the same time dismayed for all those lies that kept you in ignorance and the time wasted. This is the valley of disillusionment. At the same time you are overtaken by sadness. You feel liberated, yet like coming out of prison after spending a lifetime there, you are overtaken by a deep sense of depression. You feel lonely and, despite your freedom, you miss something. You ponder the time lost. You think of the many people who believed in this nonsense and foolishly sacrificed everything for it, including their lives. The pages of history are written with the blood of people who were killed in the name of Yahweh, Allah, or other gods. All for nothing! All for a lie!

That's when you enter the sixth valley: anger. You become angry at yourself, and at everything else. You realize how much of your precious life you lost believing in so many lies.

Then you realize you are the lucky one for having made it this far and that there are billions of others who are still trying to shield themselves with denials and not venture out of their comfort zone. They are still wading in the quagmire of the first valley. At this stage, when you are completely free from faith, guilt, and anger, you are ready to understand the ultimate truth and unravel the mysteries of life. You are filled with empathy and compassion. You are ready to be enlightened. The enlightenment comes when you realize that the truth is in love and in our relationship with our fellow human beings and not in a religion or a cult. You realize that Truth is a pathless land. No prophet or guru can take you there. You are there already.

Chapter Six

AN UNTOLD LOVE STORY

"There was a ceremony, but it was not her wedding. She was dressed in white, but that was not her wedding gown. Lots of people came to the party, but they came to curse her and to throw stones at her. No music was played and no merry songs were sung; only screams of Allah-u-Akbar *filled the air."*

SINCE SEPTEMBER 11, we have continually heard that Islam is a peaceful religion. Yet the actions of hundreds of thousands of fanatical Muslims have certainly provided good cause for us to think otherwise. If we move away from the headlines, there are also untold stories that never make the news, yet reveal a dark side of Islam. For while it is most certainly true that there are many peaceful people within Islam, there are many who are not.

In the following tragic story, you will meet Yagmur, who recounts how her sister fell in love with a young man whose parents forbade him to marry her. Yagmur remembers how happy their young faces were and how in love they were. In order to obtain permission to marry from their parents, Yagmur's sister and her boyfriend told of her pregnancy. What transpires in this real-life story of heartbreak and torture is unimaginable to most of us in the West. Upon hearing about his daughter's pregnancy, Yagmur's father in a rage took her sister to the religious elders. There it was ruled that since adultery had been committed, Yagmur's sister would be sentenced to death by stoning. It is a tragic story of love with unimaginable brutality at its core. The setting of this saga may come as a surprise to many. Rather than taking place in Saudi Arabia, Iran, or Afghanistan, the setting is Turkey—which many today believe should soon become a permanent member of the European Union.

An Untold Love Story

My name is Yagmur (it means "rain"). I was born in rural Turkey, in a village. Generally, Turkish women enjoy many freedoms that our Arab sisters can't even think of. Rural Turkey is a different story. Honor killings take place every day, women don't have much say (if any) in household matters, and female employment is out of the question. However, much hard work is done by women because men don't want to strain themselves. Women are actually like cattle or slaves. If a husband tells you to do something, you have to obey.

My mother was a fairly educated woman; she taught me at home and I even went to school. My hobby was reading books. Through them I learned different languages and acquired a lot of knowledge.

I was a disciplined and obedient girl, unlike my sister who was somewhat uppity. When she was eighteen, she fell in love with a young man. They both loved each other, but he was meant for another girl, thus his parents had decided. Dating is utterly forbidden in Islam; marriages are arranged and often young people meet on their wedding day.

My sister was rebellious. She "dated" that young man. Every night she would go to see him. They even kissed and then their relationship went too far: She got pregnant. At first they planned to run away to a big city where they would be safe. They knew religious rules in villages and realized they could be in trouble. Authorities don't care what's going on in rural Turkey. Sometimes *imams, mullahs,* and elders who try to practice *Sharia* and break the secular state law are punished. But usually authorities are more interested in big cities full of tourists and turn a blind eye to what happens in villages.

I remember their young faces. I didn't understand the whole situation; I was a little girl. But when I looked at them I could see they were happy. Their happiness made me happy, too, and I wanted to smile.

Instead of eloping, they decided to speak to my father. Pregnancy is a very good reason to get permission for marriage, or so they thought.

Alas, my sister had miscalculated my father's love for her and his obsession with his religion. He became furious. Instead of letting the two young lovers marry and build their nest of love, he took her to the religious elders and they ruled that she had committed adultery. She was sentenced to death by stoning. They showed no mercy even for her unborn child. She had stained the "honor" of the family and the only way to remove that stain was to nip her life in the bud. Her unborn baby was a stain, too, and that little creature had to be destroyed as well so my family could live honorably.

In the evening before her execution, she came to my room and told me that she would miss me. She was crying and hugged me to her bosom. Then she smiled and said that soon she would see her unborn baby. I was blissfully unaware of her fate, but I felt that something bad was about to happen. I was so scared!

I still remember her black eyes; she stared at the sky while she was dug into the ground. She was wrapped in white sheets and her hands were tied to her body. She was buried up to her waist. The rabid mob circled her with stones in their hands and started throwing them at her while the roars of *Allah-u-Akbar! Allah-u-Akbar!* added to their frenzy. She twitched with pain as the stones hit her tender body and smashed her head. Blood gushed out from her face, cheeks, mouth, nose, and eyes. All she could do was to bend to the left and to the right. Gradually the movements slowed down and finally she stopped moving even though the shower of the stones did not stop. Her head fell on her chest. Her bloodied face remained serene. All the pain had gone. The hysterical mob relented and the chant of *Allah-u-Akbar* stopped. Someone approached and, with a big boulder in his hand, smashed the skull of my sister to finish her off. There was no need for that; she was already dead. Her bright black eyes that beamed with life were shut. Her jovial laughter that filled the world around her was silenced. Her heart that beat with such a heavenly love for only a short time had stopped. Her unborn baby was not given a chance to breathe one breath of air. He (or she) accompanied his young mother in her solitary and cold tomb, or who knows, maybe to a better place where love reigns and pain and ignorance are not known. These two budding lives had to be nipped so my father could keep his honor.

She wanted to marry a man whom she loved. She dreamt of wearing a white wedding dress; that there would be a big ceremony, lots of people would be invited and they all would congratulate her, chant merry songs, and throw flowers and confetti at her. Yes, there was a ceremony, but it was not her wedding. She was dressed in white, but that was not her wedding gown. Lots of people came to the party, but they came to curse her and to throw stones at her. No music was played and no merry songs were sung; only screams of *Allah-u-Akbar* filled the air. The only hug she got was from the cold earth in which she was half buried. The only kisses that she received were from the rocks thrown at her that tore her flesh and broke her bones. They were the kisses of death. She was not united with the man whom she loved but was wed to death.

This was a tragedy for my sister's young lover. His life lost its meaning. He got lashes but nothing more. He could well forget about the whole affair and get along with his life, but he didn't. I recall seeing him standing in front of our house every day, as if waiting for my sister to come out and meet him. I could see him crying. I can only imagine that when he was not crying in front of our house he was in the cemetery, crying over the grave of his love and his baby. One day he could no more bear his pain and hanged himself.

His death was hushed and no one talked about it. Maybe no one cared. He was reunited with his love and his baby. No one can hurt them anymore. No one can separate them from one another again.

It is a sad story. But unlike the story of Romeo and Juliet, it is a story that is never told. No one talks about those young lovers. No one sheds tears for them. Not only were they buried, their memories were also buried as if they never existed—their tender love was a shame to others—a shame that had to be washed with blood.

But the saddest part is that, according to Islam, my sister deserved that death. The elders were sure she would be burning in hell for eternity. No, I can't imagine that God can send someone to hell for loving and for being happy. I can't accept a cruel God.

When I turned eighteen, I was married off to a Turkish businessman from Germany. When I came to Germany I found out that he had another wife.

He is not a bad man at all. He is very kind, but he is a Muslim. He doesn't understand why Europeans don't like polygamy, for instance. He doesn't allow us to leave the home. He protects our honor in this strange way.

Then we moved to the U.K. Here we are even more isolated than in Germany because there are fewer Turks. In Germany, we at least could meet our fellow expats.

As for my relationship with my husband's first wife, we are friends. There is some rivalry between us, that's for sure. But I am alone and can't meet anyone or leave home. Her life is just as dull and empty as mine. We can't hate each other; we should be friends to overcome our troubles. My co-wife and I are like two cellmates. We only have each other. There is not much room for antagonism or hard feelings.

I have five children; she has four. She occupies a more privileged position within our family because she has a son. I have given birth only to daughters so far.

We are both educated, but she is so obsessed with kids that she has given herself up. I am still trying to grasp at nonexistent straws; probably one day I will be freed.... I read books, keep myself informed, and like to think. She is not remotely interested in reading books or thinking. I am alone.

Sometimes I think of running away, but I have five daughters. I can neither leave them, nor run away with them. I am stuck.

Even though I left Islam a long time ago, I cannot stop praying or fasting. My husband keeps a rod for the disobedient.

When I try to protest, my mouth is shut up with quotes from the Qur'an. Islam defines our lives. Isn't it stupid that people live according to a book written a long time ago?

I am not whining about my life. But I do hate Islam. At least I could object to certain traditions, but Islam preserved the worst in our culture, reducing women into slavery and keeping them ignorant. What can you expect from an uneducated woman?

When I look at my daughters, I pray that they may live in a free world, free from Islam and this slavery.

Yagmur Dursun is a pen name. Some details of this story have been changed to hide the identity of the author.

CHAPTER SEVEN

I AM AN EX-MUSLIM AND PROUD OF IT!

"I remember being taught to hate (not directly so, of course) by instilling fear against "those evil Jews," and my teachers attempting to lure me into jihad *by promising the seventy-two* Huur Al-Ay *(virgins in paradise). Of course, I was never drawn into that: I'm gay."*

FOR MANY FORMER MUSLIMS, the level of hate and rhetoric towards so-called "infidels" or *kafirs* is simply too great. Indeed, for many young Muslims who have been exposed to Western freedoms, such suppression becomes unbearable. Tragically, this sort of tyranny is no longer confined to Islamic lands, but can be found in major Western cities. Take, for example, the case of Nissar Hussein, a former Muslim in Bradford, England, who, according to the *London Times,* has been a victim of a three-year campaign of hate for leaving Islam. His family has been "jostled, abused, and attacked."[1] The family has also been asked to move out of their neighborhood. All of this, not because of what Hussein believes, but because he no longer believes in Islam. It is sadly true that such stories are becoming more frequent throughout Britain and in other parts of the world.

In the testimony you will read here, another apostate tells of his disdain for his former culture and his desire to expose its dark side—but with a sense of fear of the consequences of doing so. Indeed, it is easy to understand where that fear comes from, and why. No one—even in the West—is safe from the violence of Islam.

Former Muslim

I'm not going to give details of my personal life (my original country, family history, and so on), but suffice it to say I come originally from a Muslim country where you'd least expect to meet an ex-Muslim. Also, I am an Arab, still haven't passed the age of twenty, and I am here to share my story.

Detailing my experiences as I know them from the vantage point of nineteen years spent as a Muslim is by no means an easy task. Coming from a religious Muslim background, I was taught to believe that the Qur'an was inerrant, that Mohammad's words were to be respected, and that any form of defiance or criticism would be met with severe repercussions. I was thus forced into Islam against my will, so to speak, and I was forced to grow up with it and stick to it and was never allowed to question it.

But for the longest time I've been secretly questioning my "beliefs"; the beliefs that I grew up with and constituted who I was; the beliefs that were a great part of my identity. I remember being taught to hate (not directly so, of course) by instilling fear against "those evil Jews" and my teachers attempting to lure me into *jihad* by promising the seventy-two *Huur Al-Ay* (virgins in paradise). Of course, I was never drawn into that: I'm gay.

Regardless of how numerous we, as ex-Muslims, are, it's still hard to communicate and share this experience. It was a lonely period after my departure from Islam. I went through depression, sadness, torment, and solitude. To be out of touch with the reality and way of life around you is truly an isolating feeling. Even in calling out, finally, for help, I suddenly felt as though I were shouting into the wind.

It was just so hard to believe in a religion that forbids pre-marital sex, yet whose sacred texts explain how you should have sex in far more detail than even Carrie Bradshaw on *Sex and the City* would feel comfortable speaking about. It was hard to believe in a religion that forbids happiness, subjugates women, and treats Jews and Christians like one-thousandth-class citizens.

The more I saw the *imams* screaming and yelling and crying and whining over our "poor conditions" and using that to justify hatred and hostility towards the West, the more I was convinced

that leaving Islam would be a right choice, because no true religion could teach someone to be this hateful. Yes, there are hateful
individuals in Christianity, too; but they're so insignificant
they're often dismissed, and moreover, they do not lead prayers
in prominent and well-known mosques, or have any religious or
moral authority like these *imams* do.

So there I was; not so long ago I gave up this set of beliefs,
and I've never felt happier. I feel free, ecstatic, and joyful. I am
so thankful for people like Wafa Sultan, who showed me the
light of a religion I blindly followed. I am an ex-Muslim now, an
agnostic and probably on my way to atheism and secular hu-
manism. I left this evil part of my past behind, and it will never
make a comeback. Not ever.

I am an ex-Muslim and I am so proud of it.

CHAPTER EIGHT

A JOURNEY TO ENLIGHTENMENT

"The more I read the Qur'an; the more I realized that the book cannot be from God... I am free now. Free from fear. A religion should give mankind a reason to live. Islam gives reasons to die."

THE DECISION TO BELIEVE should be as respected as much as the resolve not to. While many people will be shocked and horrified by some of the statements in this book, for many others they ring true. It is a truth they have lived and want to share. Asad tells his story not to shock, but to reveal his experience. It is an experience that changed his life and his way of thinking. Like many students, Assad found inspiration from his college professor. But when his mentor criticized Islam, he saw how his fellow students had zero tolerance for those who would not embrace Islam wholeheartedly. This is indeed replicated in the harsh and hostile reactions we have seen on a global scale to other perceived criticisms of Islam. To most of us in the West, cartoons are a source of amusement. Sometimes they cross the line of political correctness, but in tolerant societies we have learned to accept that people are free to spin a different side to every story. Indeed, most of us in the West, if really offended by what we read in the newspaper, have the ability to complain to the editor of the publication and sometimes take legal action.

It therefore came as a surprise to many that when a Danish newspaper reprinted cartoons of the Prophet Mohammad, a Holy War would be waged not only against the offending publication but against Denmark, and that lives would ultimately be lost in the fight. Indeed, it is hard to comprehend that as a result of the cartoons' publication, Saudi Arabia would recall its ambassador to Denmark, Libya would close its embassy, Iran's president would order the cancellation of all contracts with any country which republished the cartoons, and in Gaza Scandinavians would be given forty-eight hours to leave. However, given that this was the reaction to the publication of the cartoons, then it is not too difficult to understand the mindset that hurt Asad so terribly. It is indeed not necessarily because he agreed with his college professor, but he respected his opinion and felt that he was worthy of greater appreciation by his fellow students and certainly should not have been a victim of hate.

Not all people born into Islam accept it. This story reminds us all that people in the East can leave the iron bonds of Islam behind. But the story also points out the obvious—Islam does not allow free thought.

Asad's Testimony

My journey to enlightenment started when I was a final year medical student. One day, as I was praying in the restroom of my college, one of my professors entered the room. He was sitting there and looking at me praying. When I finished, he said, "Son, can I give you some advice?"

I replied, "Okay, sir."

Then he said something which I will remember forever. These were his exact words: "Don't waste your time kissing the floor. Islam is a scam. It is a madman's ideology of hate. Qur'an is nothing but a book of baloney."

I was shocked. This professor is a very nice man. Most students liked him. He even took extra hours to teach us. Out of all professors, I liked him the most. I was thinking, *how can he say that?* I just kept quiet and walked out of the room.

Later that day, I told my roommate about it. He said it was common knowledge that the professor was an atheist. My roommate told me how much he hated this professor. I was dumbfounded. My roommate always saw him to ask his help in studies, yet he hated him. Then I told myself that I had to save this man from hell. I thought if I understood Islam deeply, I would be able to explain to him the truth of Islam. I bought a Qur'an translation by Yusuf Ali and a translation of Sahih Bukhari. That was the turning point in my life. The more I read the Qur'an, the more I realized that the book cannot be from God. The verse on slavery finally broke the shell. I am free now. Free from fear. A religion should give mankind a reason to live. Islam gives reasons to die.

Unfortunately, before I could tell this professor about my enlightenment, he died of a heart attack. It was a sad day for me. I was the only "Muslim" who attended his funeral. All other Muslim students I met told me that he is going to hell. What kind of God can condemn such a great man to hell? What is sure is that Muslims have made my life a living hell. Writing to you is the only spiritual luxury I have in an Islamic country.

CHAPTER NINE

WHY I WILL NOT EMULATE ISLAM'S PROPHET

"Muslims are quite eloquent on familial values and keen to find fault with others, especially the West. However, I challenge any Muslim to show me any virtue in their Prophet's familial life that can be blindly followed."

ON SEPTEMBER, 1, 2004, the festive beginning of a new school year in Russia turned into a national tragedy in what would become known as Russia's September 11. This was the day when a group of about thirty armed men and two women wearing explosive belts seized a secondary school in the small town of Beslan. Teachers, pupils, and their relatives were taken hostage. Their number reached about thirteen hundred and consisted mostly of children. The hostage takers demanded the withdrawal of Russian troops from neighboring Chechnya. Russian commandos and local militia surrounded the school. In a bloody assault that ensued on September 3, most hostages were freed, but in the fighting the school was destroyed, leaving most of the terrorists, eleven Russian soldiers, and over three hundred civilians killed, and many others injured. While this attack was clearly geared towards children, let us not forget all the other children who have been left orphaned in the countless other attacks that have taken place in every area of the world.

Here Divyan dedicates his testimony to those innocent children massacred in Beslan, Russia. While many in the Islamic world claim that acts of terrorism can be justified by Western foreign policy, the slaughter of these hundreds of innocent little lambs caused many to rethink radical Islam's claims. This story reveals how Divyan has now found himself in Buddhism and his testimony offers an invitation "for any Muslim to show me any virtue in their Prophet's familial life that can be blindly followed." At Beslan, children were sacrificed on the altar of Islamic terrorism. In the male-dominated world of Islam, women and children don't matter much.

Divyan's Testimony

First of all, is it necessary to say something about me? I don't like to remember my bitter past, when I was a prestigious Muslim. Like any typical ignorant Muslim, I was very much Islam-oriented. I was a man who couldn't tolerate any brickbat on his beliefs and learned to be suspicious and prejudicial against critics and criticism. I suspended all allegations brought by critics with much contempt and disdain. I, too, believed Islam's Prophet was a man of exalted morals; I was taught to live like him, to love him, and to walk on this earth just like him. All those were acceptable until I learned to doubt and to start to look upon things differently.

I learned history from an Islamic perspective, but after the completion, a simple thought provoked me to see: how could this same story be if I rewrote it from another perspective? I think it was the beginning of my enlightenment. I refused to play the part of a victim any more and a lot of courage was needed for the purpose.

I don't exactly remember what wrote doubt in my mind. Maybe it is Lord Buddha and his teachings or a glance at Jesus and his sufferings. I learned to look into my own inner self through Buddha. Then, quite shockingly, I realized my beloved Prophet is a misfit. He failed to show me anything other than the dark side of human nature.

Those who trumpet the greatness of Islam's Prophet have a responsibility to prove it by referring to him and his life. Is there any lesson of mercy in Islam's Prophet that can be compared with what Jesus showed to his executioners even in the excruciating pain of crucifixion? Where is the moral of renunciation in him when we have Lord Buddha as a role model of ultimate renunciation?

Muslims are quite eloquent on familial values and keen to find fault with others, especially the West. However, I challenge any Muslim to show me any virtue in their Prophet's familial life that can be blindly followed.

I left this Prophet and his teachings, but this is not a praise-worthy act, when I should be ashamed of being a part of this cult at least for quite some period of my life in the past. A repentance and apology is due. So let me try my best.

I dedicate this testimony to the whole of suffering humanity; I dedicate this to those innocent kids massacred in Beslan. Shame on you, Muslims; you still taste their blood sweet!

CHAPTER TEN

AN AMERICAN WOMAN CONVERTS TO ISLAM

"I was introduced to my future husband. I was simply led into a room and told that he was the man that I was supposed to marry, Muhammad. I had no choice in the matter. We married in May. I soon entered hell."

NOT ALL OF THE PEOPLE included in this book were born into Islam. However, as we will see, many who convert face problems. Mary grew up a Christian in the United States and converted to Islam in 1991. Upon her conversion, Mary sincerely believed she had found the true path. However, like countless other women, she now remembers how her life began to fall apart after her conversion. Mary explains her own personal horror story and offers a warning to any woman who is contemplating conversion. Islam remains the easiest religion to join but the most difficult to leave and remain alive; especially for women. And if Islam ever takes hold in the West, Mary will not be alone—other women will pay the price, too.

Mary's Testimony

Some of my earliest memories revolve around church. I was taken to many church-related activities from the time that I was a little girl. However, as I grew up, my family attended less and less often and soon we spent Sundays watching television and at other leisure activities. Yet, when I was nine, my family began attending a small, independent church which was heavy on doctrine. The rhetoric included such beliefs as "spare the rod, spoil the child," and "wives, obey your husbands." They never mentioned any responsibility on the husbands' or parents' part. Consequently, I was really frightened when I went to school, church, and Sunday school and believed I would either be whipped or shamed. They would not let the girls lead the flag salute or pray since girls were supposedly less than boys. We only went to that church for a few months, but it made a huge impact on my life.

After a major move when I was twelve years old, we began attending church regularly again. I recall being happy to feel a part of a "church family," but what I did not see at the time was this was one of those churches known for "having a form of Godliness but denying the power within." I attended regularly, even though my parents began to attend less and less. Soon I was the only one from my family attending. I listened to the pastor's stories of goodness and faith, but they never really made sense, especially when the members of the congregation were involved in lying, cheating on each other, and showing off who had the most money. By the time I graduated from high school I was attending only sporadically at best.

I went away to college in 1990 and began to live my life as an agnostic, radical feminist. I did not want to believe anything that religion had to say about women being submissive. After a relationship that I was in fell apart, I began to turn back to God and religion in general. A large group of Muslim students began attending the university around this time and I began to talk to them about the way of life called Islam. They told me that Islam was a way of life and not simply a religion. I became fascinated by all the aspects and more and more interested in the fact that Muslim men were duty bound to take care of and treat their wives with care and gentleness. I was told that the Prophet Mohammad told his followers that "the best of you is the one who is the best to his wife," but no one told me about the *Surah* that states that if your wife is disobedient, you may beat her until she obeys. I wanted a good husband who would support me and treat me right.

I became a Muslim in November of 1991 and soon things began to fall apart in my life. I was so convinced that I had found the proper path that I became belligerent to my co-workers and was soon fired. I began to look for another job and was told by the *imam* that I had to return to my parents' home since Islam forbids single women from living alone. I moved home in January of 1992. Understandably, my parents did not like the idea of me wearing the traditional Muslim garb and they tried to forbid me from wearing it every chance they got. This only made me more adamant about wearing it. Soon my family and former friends were all reluctant to be around me and I spent more and more time exclusively with Muslims.

In February of 1992, I was introduced to my future husband. I was simply led into a room and told that he was the man that I was supposed to marry, Muhammad. I had no choice in the matter. We married in May. I soon entered hell. I was not to leave the apartment without his permission and was not to turn the air conditioner on under any circumstances. This was during one hundred-degree weather in the summer. I sweltered my way through the rest of the summer with heat rash and an eventual case of heat exhaustion. Muhammad forced me to relinquish control of my car to my parents in September, so I was truly stuck at home. What I did not understand about my new husband was that he would spend inordinate amounts of time away from home and never ask me to go with him. I soon learned (painfully) that Islam forbids listening to music. That was the first time that he hit me.

After our first year of marriage, he was preparing to return to Morocco (without me) to visit his family. Shortly before he left, we had been on a day trip to Dallas where he had not allowed me to have any food except a small bag of chips. As we did not have anything in the house to eat, I called one of his friends who knew that Muhammad often left me without anything to eat.

I waited for him to bring me just a small sandwich for dinner when Muhammad came home unexpectedly. He had heard of the call and was furious. He told me to get my stuff together and leave the next day. He began to beat me and scream at me, rupturing one of my eardrums. I ran to a friend's house to gain help. Muhammad tearfully apologized and we stayed together.

After he returned from Morocco, I was able to get a job and was able to pay some of my bills and have enough to eat (he let me have my car back). However, I began to understand that this was no marriage. We were simply roommates and one was terrorizing the other.

I began to question some of the things about Islam: the hypocrisy and infighting as well as the treatment of women. I was abruptly informed that I was not to question and all that I had to do was to read and I would understand. I began to look longingly at women who did not have to wear the heavy, oppressive clothing and endure the rude looks from others. I was accused of causing a miscarriage with the evil eye since I was trying desperately to become pregnant. I would cry and ask God why he would not let me achieve the supreme Muslim woman's duty of bearing children. I became more and more depressed and even prayed for God to take me out of this world. Little did I know that he would answer my prayer in a way that I had not dreamed of.

At the end of the third year of our marriage, Muhammad decided that he needed to go to Morocco again. He told me that he did not care where I went or what I did; he was going home. Well, I got my own apartment and when I did not hear from him in a month, I filed for divorce. My faith was destroyed and my health and finances were also destroyed. After many tears, I wandered back into a church. It has taken many months, but I finally feel at home.

Chapter Eleven

THE LIE: A TRUE STORY OF SAUDI WOMEN

"It is the Islamic laws in Saudi Arabia which have rendered our women chattels of men, forced them into their servitude, and have completely robbed their dignity, honor, and respect they deserve as women. To say the least, Islam has shaken and shamed the very basic foundation of womanhood."

ONE OF THE MOST disconcerting aspects of Islam is its treatment of women. Nowhere is this more rampant than in Islamic countries. In order to understand Walid's story it is important to comprehend what life is like for women in Saudi Arabia. Indeed, while the lashings of women as punishment has sparked international outrage, it is still very difficult for many to fully comprehend what further suppression women endure in the Kingdom. In fact, nowhere is this more evident than by the Kingdom's laws and views towards women. For it is sadly true that even driving a car is forbidden for women in Saudi Arabia; although in January 2008, a new rule enabling women to stay alone in a hotel room was brought into effect. However, by and large women have no rights whatsoever and to best understand this it is important to understand the Kingdom itself. Why do so many Western nations remain allied with Saudi Arabia and why is the Saudi king entertained in Buckingham Palace and at Camp David?

Women have few if any rights in Saudi Arabia. At McDonald's, women order from one side of a divided counter and disappear with their value meals into the walled-off "family section." Men order on the other side of the counter and sit in plain view of everyone.

Indeed, because Saudi Arabia is a conservative Islamic country with no movie theaters, bars, or discos, Saudis tend to spend a lot of time hanging out at the mall. Yet for all their Western-style glitz, it seems that Riyadh's malls also reflect Saudi culture, which mandates that women be covered—even on CDs—and that the sexes remain largely segregated.

Even trying on clothes is difficult for Saudi women who have to put down a deposit and take garments to the women's rest rooms. Yet, while reforms to change segregation are underway, Saudi Arabia still remains one of the most conservative, some say repressive, societies in the world.

Why should this be of concern to us in the West? Aside from the issue of the violation of human rights, the way current trends are moving, soon this may be happening not far away! In truth, as Muslim populations grow within Western countries, so too will the cry for Islamic laws to be instated.

Life is far from easy for Saudi women, who for the most part remain the property of men and have to abide by strict Saudi rules. Women are frequently confined to their homes or the homes of their female friends. Often, the only connection these women have to the outside world is via the Internet. For unless they are with a relative or spouse, women in Saudi Arabia cannot visit a man's home and certainly cannot be seen with him in public. In essence, women in Saudi Arabia are segregated to second-class citizenship. When they marry they may have to do so to someone who has been chosen for them. If they don't marry, they can be frowned upon. It is in light of these injustices that continue in Saudi Arabia that Whalid offers testimony about the struggles challenging his own sisters within the Kingdom.

Next, you will read Whalid's chilling account of how Islam can turn a father against his own daughters. Islam allows this—even encourages it. And that's all the more reason why we must stand firm against the oppressive Islamic way of life imposing itself on Western culture.

Whalid's Testimony

Many people have said that Islam respects women and values them. But, from my own experience, I have found this to be just a fat lie. As a native of Saudi Arabia, I have personally witnessed how despicably women are treated in our Islamic society. In this testimony I shall narrate my experience of such oppressive and horrific treatment of our women, *a la* Islam. Every word that I am going to write is absolutely true—nothing has been fabricated or exaggerated. No one coerced me to write this story, because I am born a Saudi and I live right here in Saudi Arabia.

I have three sisters. They were highly motivated to be educated, and by their own effort, pursued modern education. But because of many absurd, outdated, and unfair impediments imposed on women's education in our society, they could not finish their chosen fields of learning. Despite my sincere intention, I could simply do nothing to help them get proper education. My hands were tied; our society frowns upon women who are highly educated in a modern way.

One of my sisters finished secondary school, and then she stopped studying because she was keen on beauty training. But in a pure Islamic society like ours, it is not that easy for her to pursue her ambition to be a beauty therapist.

My other two sisters wanted to be schoolteachers. So they continued with their studies and finished their Higher Secondary Level.

I clearly remember that when they were in the college, their identification cards were in their own names, but the photographs on the cards were that of my father! This meant my sisters had no physical existence—they existed in name only—on a piece of paper. Readers, please do not be shocked at such an appalling treatment of our women—they are just like domestic animals—always owned by someone. They could not subsist on their own as human beings. The law in Saudi Arabia, vis-à-vis women, stipulates that no girl/woman in a college could insert her own photograph in her identity card; instead, only the photograph of her father, brother, husband, or her *mahram* (guardian) must be attached.

Anyway, after finishing their teachers' training, these two sisters of mine had to wait for jobs which must be in the vicinity of their dwelling. They cannot go away from my father's control. If they dared to do so, they would never get jobs.

As a conscientious brother, I firmly believe that my sisters are wise and responsible—more than many men in my area, even more than me. I am certain that given the chance to live and manage their lives by themselves, they would succeed without any problems. In fact, they are capable of accomplishing far more difficult tasks than many of us could.

But alas! These three educated, wise, responsible, and ambitious girls are held prisoners at home by their illiterate father. He does not know anything about the world outside of home. He sees no need at all for any progress or development of civilization. And he has forced my sisters to live his periphery of life.

This illiterate father banned them (my sisters) from getting married. It was because of his strict demand for non-smoking, strictly Islamic bridegrooms from the same tribe which he belongs to. It looks like such dim-witted demands might keep my sisters spinsters for the foreseeable future.

In our society of strict Islamic adherence, all men who are smokers and/or do not pray regularly in mosques are considered unfit for marriage. As a binding rule, a man who is considering getting married must produce at least two witnesses who would vouch that the prospective bridegroom regularly prays in a mosque. This condition is so important in Saudi society that failure to produce such witnesses might result in the breakup of the proposed marriage. More importantly, a Saudi woman from one tribe must not marry a man from another tribe or from another nationality, even though the man is a Muslim. Forget about a Saudi woman marrying a non-Muslim—this is *haram*.

In our tribe the girls outnumber the boys two or three times. This means that many of our girls will never get married, as marrying outside of our tribe is absolutely unthinkable. In our society men prefer to marry girls less than twenty years old. They have a special penchant for girls who are around sixteen years or less. The conclusion from this absurd desire for very young girls is that the marriage prospect of girls more than twenty years old is almost zero. Or, they might get married, but to older men.

Thus, because of these ridiculous Islamic rules, the lives of these grown-up girls mean nothing in our puritanical society.

Let us now return to my father's mentality and find the real reason why he does not want his daughters to be married to strangers (I mean, men from another tribe or another nationality).

Saudi men strongly believe that women have no hopes, desires, and aspirations of their own. Thus, when it comes to marriage, a Saudi woman's opinion is irrelevant. She is totally dependent on her owner about her fate. Saudi men also consider it shameful to give someone's daughter to be married to a stranger—outside one's own tribal boundary. It is difficult for a Saudi man to accept that outsiders could look at the sacred "honor" of their daughters. It is inconceivable for a Saudi father to envisage that a stranger could have sex with his daughter— even in marriage, and even when the bridegroom is a Muslim. So, this is the real reason why my father would not allow my sisters to marry "foreigners." He is simply paranoid that "foreigners" would have sexual intercourse with his daughters.

For the reasons stated above, many Saudi fathers ask for double marriages—that is: give me your daughter and I will give you my daughter or sister…and so on. In this way, they feel comfortable: We will protect his honor if he protects ours. This is how people in our society use women for their own benefit—when they need money, or when they need new wives. There are some Saudi women who earn wages, but the money they get goes to the pockets of their fathers or husbands. For fear that their daughters' salaries might be appropriated by their husbands, many Saudi fathers do not want their daughters married. To me, this might be another reason why my father has literally put a ban on the marriage of my sisters.

So how do my sisters live in this society?

As Saudi women, my sisters go through extraordinary suffering. They have no right whatsoever to manage their lives by themselves. They are totally dependent on my father, on me, and on their other brothers. They cannot go anywhere alone. Whenever any one of them ventures outside, some man (brother or father) must accompany her as her protector and minder. They cannot even go out for such events like an accident, hospital emergency, etc. Believe me, when they need to go to a hospital, they have to call my brother to take them there. He has to come from another city, three hundred kilometers away. Because they cannot drive (women in Saudi Arabia are banned from driving cars and are not allowed to go with non-*mahram*) and my father cannot drive, my sisters have no choice but to undergo such unspeakable ordeals of agony. No matter how urgent their case, they must wait for their *mahram* (in this case, their brother) to take them to the hospital.

There is no way out for them. Since my father does not know how to use an ATM, when any of my sisters wants to withdraw money from an ATM, she must hand over her card to a stranger (a man) to withdraw money for her. When my sisters want to do regular shopping, they must hand over the money to a stranger and he will charge whatever price he wishes. These are just a few examples of the plights Saudi women go through in their daily lives.

Sometimes I do think to leave my job, just to stay with them.

So, you might say: Why not take them out of Saudi Arabia? This is utterly impossible. In Saudi Arabia, to secure a passport, a woman must have the written permission from her *mahram* (father, brother, or husband). Obtaining a passport is not enough for a Saudi woman to travel alone. Her father (in case she is unmarried) must sign special papers to permit her to go on a voyage on her own. Being illiterate, my father will never allow his daughters to leave Saudi Arabia; I am absolutely certain of this.

Sometimes, I really wonder why such an unbearable torment has been imposed on our women. My sisters cannot do anything without the permission and assistance of my father or brother. They are at home, all the time, watching television. There is no sport for them to play, no work to attend to, no hope, and nothing to live for. They are incarcerated in the biggest prison in the world—Saudi Arabia, the land of pure, unadulterated Islam.

One might legitimately ask: Why do all these things happen to Saudi women? Who is to be blamed for this loathsome ordeal perpetrated on our women? It is quite easy to blame the silly, in-ane Saudi laws, the widespread illiteracy prevalent among the Saudi people, and the archaic traditions for the hopeless condi-tion of our women. But think again. All these factors are firmly rooted in Islam. It is Islam which is clearly the culprit. It is the Islamic laws in Saudi Arabia which have rendered our women chattels of men, forced them into their servitude, and have com-pletely robbed their dignity, honor, and respect they deserve as women. To say the least, Islam has shaken and shamed the very basic foundation of womanhood.

Islam provides complete authority to a father to control his daughters. He has full control to give them in marriage, to ban them from social life, or even to kill them. You might be shocked to learn that a Saudi father can kill his daughter with complete impunity. Please know that even when he kills his daughter, the government will not kill the father because she is his probity. Ac-cording to *Sharia*, the government is not allowed to kill a father if he kills his daughter or son for any reason.

In Islam, a daughter cannot marry without her father's per-mission—it is *haram*. In a nutshell, in Islam, a father is a holy man, a commander, and a petulant dictator. Even when he is illit-erate, obdurate, unjust, and insensible, his children, especially the daughters, can do nothing against him.

So, in my case, what can I do?

The straightforward answer to this question would be: noth-ing. I can do virtually next to nothing to change the situation. If I file a case against my father, the religious judge will ask him, "Why don't you let your daughters get married?" My father's vague answer will be, "These girls are my responsibility (that is, under my safe custody), and Allah will punish me if I don't choose good husbands for them." As a proof of his sincere effort he might even produce evidence that all the men he had sought were smokers and also will bring witnesses that they were also non-praying (in mosque) Muslims. This will completely persuade the Islamic judge. He will find no ground to chastise my father; instead, he might impose punishment on me for not respecting my father and his decisions.

With such anguish and frustration in my heart, I am patiently waiting for the death of my father. Once he dies, the control of my sisters will automatically transfer to me. Their ownership will officially be in my hands.

I shall be their new possessor—just like cars, houses, goats, camels, etc. Then I shall be completely free to do with them whatever I wish—Islam gives me all the authority. I could take them to hell or to heaven—wherever I desire.

Readers, please do not feel sorry or pity for my sisters. Compared to many other Saudi women, they are quite lucky— they can visit shopping centers once or twice a year. They can use makeup and they can even listen to music. The best freedom they have is that they can choose television channels they like to watch. For many Saudi women, this is a great privilege, if you did not know.

CHAPTER TWELVE

MY AWAKENING

"Islam was created by a Prophet who was indeed vile and a pedophile...If Allah is most gracious, most merciful, he wouldn't have chosen such an ill minded Prophet."

LIKE SO MANY OTHERS, Andrea converted to Islam, and while not everyone who converts has the same experience, Andrea truly believes that many do. She shares her story to warn anyone contemplating conversion of the horrors that she personally endured and she certainly feels an obligation to do so. For it seems that to fall in love with a strict Muslim means having to fully embrace every aspect of Islam, too!

They say that love is blind. In this case, Andrea's love for her husband blinded her to the harsh realities of his Islamic beliefs. Can a Westerner happily marry a Muslim? Andrea thought so. Then her dream marriage turned into a nightmare.

Andrea's Testimony

My story is like the stories of thousands of other converts. I grew up somewhat rebellious, spiritually anyway, and I hated going to church each Sunday. I was the type of person who loved learning about other people, other cultures, and other religions. When I started studying Islam, I was utterly fascinated. The books that were created for those interested in the religion showed the perfection of the religion. "To kill one man is the same as killing all of humanity." I really loved that one. (Now that I think about it, I can see the stupidity of this statement.)

I got deeply involved in studying; the sites I studied from had been delicately created by those knowing exactly what a convert hopes to find. A convert is looking for a religion that does not dispute science generally, a religion that is peaceful, and a religion based on the idea of one God. The creators of these sites know this, and they foster influence on those on a spiritual search and with a naive mind. I was indeed one on a spiritual search; I wanted to feel connected to something larger than myself, and I wanted to be surrounded by moral people, with strong convictions against immoral things. Islam was all of this for me. I became very involved in the religion, and whenever I happened to stumble upon "radical," or as I refer to them today "Islamically correct," sites, I simply said, "Those are the ones with messed up views, every religion has them, and they're ashamed of them." I found many Muslims on chat rooms, and we all united in the cause that Israel stole Palestine's land, the West was corrupt and evil, and Jews were behind all evil acts. Funny, how easily you can get convinced with eloquent words!

Then, one day I met Mohammad (no, not the pedophile who started the whole cult). This was Mohammad from Morocco, and he had come to the U.S. and was living very close to me. We discussed Islam a lot, and we were both pretty liberal; we listened to music, agreed that a woman shouldn't be forced to wear *hijab*, that if a woman wants a job it's fine, and that polygamy is outdated. I really liked that about him, so we talked every night, on voice chat, and used the webcam (major sin in Islam by the way, to talk with non-Muslims, especially while viewing the face).

We were only friends, and he actually had a fiancée back in Morocco, but he talked to me about how all she wanted to do was lay around on the beach in her bikini; we both agreed she had been corrupted by Western values, and women shouldn't show their bodies off for men to see. So eventually he broke things off with her. Yes, we decided that we were a perfect couple to get married. So he made a visit to me, and we affirmed that belief even more. I was moving to another state soon, and he also decided that he would move to be with me, and once he got himself financially secure, we would get married. Here is what was so perfect to me: He had always wanted to go back to his country and live there after finishing his education, but now, because he knew me, he was willing to give up everything that he had planned to do. How romantic, right? How could anyone ever say that Muslim guys are controlling over women?

Things continued to get better with Mo, as I called him; we began to plan our whole future. I would work in the political field, while he worked in the computer field. We would live in Connecticut (suburbs of course). I was so in love. Then one night, I said something off the topic of our future plans. I said, "I just can't get over these men who want more than one wife; I mean that's just really stupid, and demeaning towards women."

I was not just speaking of Muslims but Mormons and other primitive people who agreed with this idea. Suddenly his face changed from its usual happiness into a scornful look. He said: "How could you argue with Allah's words?" I said, "Well, in the days of Mohammad, culture was different and so he didn't see anything wrong with having more than one wife, and wars left a lot of women as widows, and they needed caregivers." I was re-hashing the prefabricated Islamic response to this question, mind-lessly. He asked me if I thought Islam was outdated. I replied, "Well, even you agree that cutting off people's heads is barbaric, and that women working can be a necessity in this society." He said, "Yes, but I do not argue that it is Allah's will. You say Allah is wrong by saying polygamy is wrong....and those who don't fully believe in all of Allah's words are *kafirs*, and *kafirs* go to hell." Wow, what a change! I immediately said my good night, and that I didn't want to talk to someone irrational like that. The next day I received a kind email, filled with regrets. That worked! Naively, I accepted his apologies and we continued on as before. I must add, I worried a lot about how I was going to finance certain aspects in my very expensive education.

I really don't know where the turning point came, but I started to become a little suspicious of some Islamic ideas as I re-searched more. Not befriending *kafirs*, MURDERING, lying, WOM-EN'S STATUS. Wow, what had I missed here? So I talked to Mo about it, and apparently, this was his boiling point. Here is the email I received from him. My words are in bold in the following paragraph.

What the hell is your problem? I am willing to give up everything for you, my country, my life, my pride...and whenever I ask you to make one sacrifice, you get scared of it, scared of Allah's will **(Note—The sacrifice he is mentioning is my disapproval of being a housewife)**. How can you dispute what Allah has laid out so clearly? You care only about money... Care? No that's not the word...You are obsessed with money just as badly as the Jews. Your dreams are not of how to worship your God, and submit to his will, but how you can make more money, and get power. When I dream, I dream of coming home to you, after a hard day of work, and I see you cooking for me, a clean house, and after that, we have our time in bed. When you dream, you dream of how you get more money, how you can get your husband to buy you what you want. That is the mind of a sick woman. **(I'm the sick one?)** Listen here, Allah says the man is more powerful than the woman, and his job is to watch over her, yet you reject all of it. Here are my demands and you will follow them not because I demand them, but because Allah demands them. And Allah demands submission to the husband.

You will wear *hijab* at all times.

You will not befriend Muslim girls without *hijab*, and you will absolutely not befriend *kafirs*.

When a male friend or colleague of mine enters the house, you will go to a separate room, and stay there until he leaves, unless you serve him food or drink.

You will not work, even if I am not able to financially support you, you will be around *kafirs* at work, and they will look at you lustfully and tempt you to do wrong. Women are weak, you are weak, and you will probably end up harrased by a *kafir*.

If you leave, even with friends, tell me where you are at all times, and whatever you buy you must show me once you return home.

I am allowed to beat you softly, but only under extreme circumstances, such as denying.

My Response:

Dear Mo,

I feel so stupid in my ignorance, in my *naiveté*, to not see the truth. You have laid out everything so perfectly for me. I guess seeing that I am a woman it is somewhat difficult to come to terms with what Islam expects from me. Islam wants me to be a housewife, Islam wants me to submit to all of your requests, Islam wants me to be completely veiled, except my face and hands. How did I miss this? I really want to thank you for bringing the truth to me, for in your email you have clearly laid out what had previously been hidden to me.

You showed me that Islam believes that women are merely sex objects and property, Islam was created by a Prophet who was indeed vile and a pedophile, Islam allows you to beat me. It allows you to be a polygamist. What does it allow me? It allows me to stay in the house, because I am nothing but an object of sin. If Allah is most gracious, most merciful, he wouldn't have chosen such an ill minded Prophet. If Allah is who we worship, and whose aid we seek, count me out! I don't seek the aid of a vengeful God, who thinks beheading people is okay, who thinks beating women is okay, who thinks pedophilia is okay in this life, and homosexual pedophilia is okay in the next.

My mother always taught me to respect those whose opinions are different, and understand that everyone has their own way of spiritual enlightenment. She also taught me to never use foul language. Most of all, never be angry, because you will later regret what you say. Sorry Mom, I guess I failed you tonight with what I am about to say.

F you! (Wow that really does feel good.) I will not serve you, and I will not serve a god who is the monster the Qur'an speaks of. Call me a *kafir*, please; I would much rather be associated with that culture, than one that believes it's okay to kill 750 Jews in one day, behead nonbelievers, and escalate an old man who had sex with a nine-year-old girl, and married her at age six. If the *jannah* you speak of is full of people like you, why would I want a destination like that? The true hell would be living around millions of people such as you.

I will lock my doors now, change my name, and move…because for Muslims to denounce Islam and leave their religion is punishable by death.

CHAPTER THIRTEEN

YOU WERE RIGHT ALL ALONG

"They told me the very word 'Islam' was 'peace.' But they lied. Now I know it means 'submission,' which is the opposite of peace. I did the world no justice when I helped to glorify Islam."

A S WE HAVE SEEN, leaving Islam is not an easy choice or a viable option. To become an apostate means not just turning one's back on your faith and your friends but in many cases even your family. It also requires questioning and ultimately denying everything you once believed in. When this realization happened to Dee Anna she felt compelled to write to Ali Sina at Faith Freedom because she began to think that he and many other fellow apostates were right all along!

One of the most important concerns raised in this book is stated clearly in this short letter by Dee Anna: Islam means submission, not peace. Dee Anna's story proves that what happened to her could happen to anyone.

Dee Anna's Testimony

I wanted so much for Islam to be good that I fell into its trap and tried to make it good. And yet I noticed my brothers and sisters in Islam, who praised me when I praised Islam, just as quickly and readily demonized me when I began to question all the lies I was told about Islam.... Because, you see, I knew nothing of Islam, nothing at all. September 11 was my first introduction to Islam.

But I was so eager to love the world into a better world. Muslims began telling me Osama was to Islam as the anti-Christ was to

Christianity; they told me Islam was all about peace and love, and that Mohammad was some great prophet of peace. They praised him as though he were pro-women. They basically made him into a god. But they did not tell me about his evil actions, and when I began to learn of them and wanted to discuss them because I still wanted to believe Islam was good and perhaps there was some good explanation for why Mohammad would commit such evils, I quickly learned that to dare question Mohammad is to be demonized, threatened, abused, etc. They will also see themselves as doing good. As a result I began to study and learn all the more, and after five or six years of research and trying so hard to prove apostates wrong, all I have found is that they were right all along.

I put some challenges of apostates before my Islamic friends as though they were my own challenges. They could not dispute them. They merely attacked and demonized me instead. The very people I worked so hard to defend became my enemies. As they demonized me, more and more I began to get angry. The more I saw the truth about Islam, the angrier I became. I was hurt, very, very hurt, afraid, shocked, and humiliated.

On one hand they tried to convert people to Islam—tried to convince people that Islam is about love and peace, but never did they show me this alleged love and peace; nor did they show this love and peace to anyone else who did not glorify Islam as they did. I started off full of love and eager to embrace Islam and be embraced by it. I defended it. I told the lies it had trained me to tell. I proclaimed Islam is peace, because that's what they told me. They told me the very word "Islam" was "peace." But they lied. Now I know it means "submission," which is the opposite of peace. I did the world no justice when I helped to glorify Islam: And now because I know the truth, the whole truth, about Islam and because of all that it has done to me and because of what it has done to believers and disbelievers alike, I hate Islam. By saying this I am often demonized and they see me only with hatred. But they do not understand. I hate Islam because I love humanity. I love the believers and the disbelievers alike and I hate what Islam has done to them, for what it has done to humanity. I hate Islam and never again will I defend it; never will I submit, or bow!

CHAPTER FOURTEEN

DISOWNED

"Allah, show me how I can be like them [have peace] in Islam...The answer never came. I finished the Qur'an and could not identify the same God. Could he be different? If Islam is right, then Christianity cannot be right."

FOR MANY WHO leave Islam, the process involves not only giving up a religion; for some it also means being disowned by family and abandoned by friends. For while Iran finds itself isolated from the international community, many Iranians have been individually isolated from family because of the way that they view the Iranian regime and how it affects their lives.

When her husband became a Christian, Sarah found herself wrestling with her own native Islam. In the end, she decided that the violence of Islamic teaching could not match the powerful grace and love of the Bible. She knows Islam. And she knows the dangers it presents. Her message to anyone reading this: Christ is peace, Islam is not. She worries that the West does not understand this. And she fears for the future.

Sarah's Testimony

I was born in Tehran, Iran, in the 1950s. I was raised in an educated and wealthy Shiite family. My father was a very devout Muslim man who loved to please God. He was very spiritually sensitive and used to always talk about faith, love, and obedience. He had previously lived on the wild side, but in his mid-thirties, after having three or four kids, he settled down and turned to God. He tried to know Allah with all of his might, and what Islam was able to give him. He also studied other religions, some in order to know if there is more to religion than what Islam offered. Unfortunately, his studies did not go deep enough into Christianity. There was not a Christian who wanted to share deeply his life in Christ with him. My father was trained by the U.S. military, so he lived in America many times, for three to eighteen months at a time. But as far as I know, no one ever witnessed to him.

I loved my dad; he was a great man. As his youngest child I looked up to him as my hero. Even though I was a girl in a Muslim country, he always gave me the type of opportunities that only male children received in that culture. When I was a teenager, he sent me to America to continue my education and become a doctor one day. I was a very good student and he wanted me to achieve the most I could in my life.

When I came here, I was surprised with the culture. It was a bit wild. It was the '70s, and some high school girls were very loose. I always had male friends, but could not date when I was in Iran. This open dating was very new to me. I did not join the dating scene until I started attending college. Of course, my parents were not aware of this side of my life. They would have never approved of it. I met many American guys; since I was a popular student in college, I got to go out on a lot of dates. But after the guys found out that the good night kiss was even a bit too much for me, they would not ask me out for a second date. While I attended college, I lived with an American family who attended church every Sunday. I even went with them. The Gospel was preached, but it had no affect on me. I believe that the Holy Spirit opens our ears and eyes when it is our time to hear his message.

I knew Alex from my high school years. He was very popular, a soccer jock, great-looking; a nice guy whom all the popular girls had dated. I met up with him two years later. We started going out together. He knew that I was a Muslim, although a nominal one at this point; he was a nominal Catholic. We began to date exclusively; he was patient enough not to push me into a type of relationship other men sought. I fell in love with him, and after dating each other for three to four months we decided to get married. We were not even twenty years old yet. We chose not to tell our parents about our decision. When his parents found out they took it a bit hard, but they knew me and liked me. Their faith was not very strong, so it did not bother them that their son had married a Muslim.

Even though I was not a practicing Muslim, I had told Alex that I would never change my religion for him. I was very proud of my heritage and my religion. He did not have any problems with that, because he did not have any more conviction in Jesus Christ than I had at that point.

When my parents found out that I had gotten married to a young high school graduate, from a Spanish heritage and a Catholic, they went crazy. My father disowned me and my mother was so angry with me that she could not even talk to me over the phone. I was so devastated. I could not cope with separation from them. What was I thinking when I married Alex? This could not work. I told Alex that if my parents didn't forgive me, I would have to leave him. It was a difficult time for us. We loved each other, but my family had to come first.

Three weeks later, I got a phone call from my dad. Yes, my dad. He and Mom were coming to America to meet my husband. I was so happy and scared at the same time. So was Alex. When they arrived and spent some time with Alex, they realized why I had married him. He was a whole lot like my dad. My dad spent many hours telling Alex about Islam. His goal in life was to convert my husband. Alex was very challenged spiritually and was very impressed with my father's knowledge and zeal toward his faith. Believe it or not, God used my Muslim father to get Alex interested in searching his faith, and finding out if Christianity had this many interesting facts about it, and what it really meant to him. Why did he call himself a Christian?

After five years of marriage, Alex was transferred to the Far East with the military. I could not go with him, and I was finishing up college. I was all alone and did not have family or any close friends nearby. Alex was making new friends at his new station, and they had asked him to start attending their church. He truly was searching to find the real meaning of his faith, and once and for all make a decision what he was going to do about it. Thousands of miles away, God started working in my life, too. He started to surround me with Christians.

I met Mary in one of my classes. She always had a big smile on her face, and showed a lot of interest in the foreign students. She and I became very good friends, and she became my sister. She had been a Catholic until recently, then she had surrendered her heart to Jesus Christ and had joined an evangelical church. For the first time in my life, I began to see what Jesus Christ can do in a person's life. She was always there for me. She never hit me over the head with her Bible, but she shared many beautiful passages from it. She was there when I needed a shoulder to cry on when I missed my husband. She was there to study with me when we were preparing for a final exam. She was there when I read Alex's letters where he explained to me his journey to find Christ. She would get so excited for him, even though she had never met him before.

A few months later, for my graduation, Alex returned home. He was a new man. He had been baptized at his church and had been "born again." I did not understand. Wasn't he a Christian before? Mary and Alex, when they met, acted like they had known each other for many years. That was odd! Alex and I took off after my graduation and took a long trip back home, so I could settle there when he returned back to the Far East.

During this long road trip, Alex shared with me his new-found faith. He truly was changed. He was very much at ease, had a peace that I could not explain. He was very confident, and very caring. He was a changed man. He told me that he would love for me to know God through Jesus Christ. I got very angry about this. I reminded him that I had vowed to stay a Muslim until I died. He was very much saddened about my comment, but he never brought up this question again. He went to God on his knees and gave me to him. Alex knew that I was too hard of a task for him alone. I was very stubborn and I would never give in to his desire. He did challenge me to at least live out my faith.

After he returned to the Far East and I got my first job and settled down, I began to pray every day, and read the Qur'an. I was searching for the peace he had found. After all, we wor-shipped the same God; he must offer the same benefits in Islam as he has done in Christianity. While I was searching in Islam for this God of love and peace, God did not stop his work in my life. The first guy I met at my new job happened to be a "born again" ex-Catholic! How could I get away from these people?

He too was very zealous in his faith, and did not hesitate to share the four spiritual laws with me. I told him to back off, because I knew what he believed and I was not interested. He now knew that God was really working on me. He was so kind; he helped me when I had car troubles. He was always there to lend me a hand in our projects. When I was in error, he would take the blame for it. He was very loving and had a peace that I could not explain. I had witnessed Mary, Alex, and now Matt. There was a lot of commonality between these folks, and they did not even know each other! *Allah, show me how I can be like them in Islam.*

The answer never came. I finished the Qur'an and could not identify the same God. Could he be different? If Islam is right, then Christianity cannot be right. *Someone is telling a lie here!* I would pray to God every night to show me the truth. I was suspicious of Islam now, with all of the hate, judgment, wrath, lies, ungodly life of the Prophet, etc. I could not believe the Christian message that I needed a savior, and that was Jesus Christ, God himself! What a strange message. *God, please show me which one is the truth!*

Eighteen months had passed since my husband had asked me to consider Christ. I was more confused and more defensive now than ever before. He had returned home for good and he found himself well challenged by me. I truly made his life miserable. There was a spiritual war in our home. I went to church with him, but did not participate in any prayers or hymn singing with the congregation. I did not believe what they were saying, so I would not take part in those activities.

I could not be convinced of the fact that Jesus was God himself. That was blasphemy! Not only did it not make sense, but it made the hair on my back stand straight. How could these people believe all of this?

After we had attended this church for four to five months, I went to a service by myself because my husband was out of town. Since I knew the pastor and many other young couples—they were our friends now—I felt comfortable enough to go by myself. That day during the altar call, I caught myself singing "Amazing Grace." I could not believe it. I stopped in the middle and would not sing anymore. The pastor asked the congregation, "If you feel that the Holy Spirit is calling you to come forward, don't hesitate."

No way was I going forward. I was emotional at that point, my husband wasn't even there, and I still did NOT believe that Jesus was God himself. The pastor waited and no one went forth. That evening when Alex came home, I did not say anything to him. The next morning, October 2, 1983, I woke up my husband and told him that I believed Jesus to be God himself, and that I needed him to forgive me for my sins, and become my savior. Alex was so shocked that he cried like a baby. He could not believe that God had changed my hardened heart toward himself. He had done the work, with the witnesses that my friends and husband had brought to me. What a joy, I was now BORN AGAIN.

CHAPTER FIFTEEN

TORTURED FOR LEAVING ISLAM

"My father delivered me to the Security Forces and they arrested me and put me in prison for converting out of Islam. I had a very bad time there, as they tortured me to force me to return to Islam."

FOR FUNDAMENTALIST followers of Islam, receiving an order to kill in God's name poses a strong challenge. Bassam chose to reject the challenge and rise up against it. Sadly, he was not only standing up to a method of government, but to his own father who handed him over to the Security Forces. His crime: He did not want to follow Islam.

Bassam shows us the real meaning of courage. He urges all of us to take a stand like he did when he took a stand against Muslim extremists—including his own family. And he also warns us: *Look at what Islam did to me.... It could do the same to you.*

Bassam's Testimony

I live in the Middle East. I was born as a Muslim, and at the age of eighteen I became a member of one of the Islamic groups, as I had a relative who was one of the leaders of this group. I thought I was doing everything I could for God as I knew him at this point.

After a short time I started to get some training in using guns and making explosives. I wasn't very comfortable with what I was doing—hurting people for God's sake. I thought that either I or the group had misunderstood the teachings of God. I started to study the Qur'an and the *Hadith* all over again (with the help of one of the leaders of the group, without telling him my real reasons for studying), to see what I had missed. After a couple of years I was astonished at what I found. I found that Islam is not the peaceful path to God, as I used to believe; on the contrary, it's so violent. *If I have to establish God's will by any means possible, even by killing people,* I said, *it can't be the way to God.*

I never considered myself leaving Islam for anything else, yet at this point I was sure that it wasn't leading me to God. I had a kind of breakdown for some time when I found that everything I had believed in wasn't right; I started doing drugs, and not talking about God at all.

Then I met a Christian who didn't know much of the Christian theology but who was full of love to others, whatever and whoever they were. One of his friends (who was a member of the same group that I had been involved in) said about him that he must be killed because he was Christian and didn't pay *Jiziah* (tax levied on Christians and Jews in an Islamic state, according to the Qur'an), yet this didn't stop him loving this man or dealing with him professionally. Initially, I didn't know he was Christian, and when I found out I was surprised; everything I had learned all my life about Christians from my reading of Islamic writings and Mohammad's opinion about them put them down very much. I asked this friend if I could have a copy of the Bible.

After starting to read the Bible, I found a very big difference between what is actually written in the Bible and what I had heard people (Muslims and even nominal Christians) say about it.

I was really struck by one thing in the Bible, namely the teaching that no one is righteous but Jesus; even those who were called God's people—like David, Jacob, and Abraham, the twelve apostles—everyone has done something wrong. The Bible is full of the sins and wrongdoing of all people, except Jesus. He himself said to his enemies, "Which of you convicts me of sin?" (John 8:46a), and no one responded. Even Judas Iscariot, who delivered him up to the authorities to be killed, said, "I have sinned in betraying innocent blood." (Matthew 27:4)

My father delivered me to the Security Forces and they arrested me and put me in prison for converting out of Islam. I had a very bad time there, as they tortured me to force me to return to Islam. They used electric shocks and beatings, and hung me from my wrists all night. After a few weeks of this I was put in solitary confinement for almost a year. But I couldn't deny the one that gave me life. Now I am out of jail and I have left my home country as I am still wanted there for apostasy from Islam.

CHAPTER SIXTEEN

A LETTER TO WESTERN INTELLIGENCE

"The motive of the Islamists is Islam—not terrorism, not Iraq, not Afghanistan. Terrorism is just a tool employed, but the Qur'an is the motivator, and Islam is the final goal. There can be no clearer message than this. The civilized world is at war—a war with Islam."

E ACH DAY in sheer despair pundits and politicians offer up endless summaries of what is happening within the world of Islam. Following the assassination of Benazair Bhutto in Pakistan, the debate concerning al-Qaeda ensued once again. Yet few seem to have any solution to stop radical Islam. Indeed, most international security agencies seem resolved that it is not a matter of *if* another major attack will happen, but *when*. Abul Kasem believes he has a solution.

Understanding Islam means understanding Islamic texts. By reading these texts, we in the West won't be surprised by the violence we see in the world. Islam does not deny its true meaning, so why should we deny it? Abul left Islam for this very reason and urges others to stay away from it.

Abul's Testimony

I am writing this testimony because it is time for us all to fully comprehend the enormity of the problem that we all confront. I have no political or theological agenda. I am, however, very concerned about the future of the free world—a world we have all seen torn apart over the past few years because of Islamic extremism. It is because of this I share my experience of Islam with you.

I have always questioned the necessity of religion in our lives and the inhumane and illogical practices in many religions, including Islam. You might wonder what triggered my distaste for religion. It all started in my schooldays when I witnessed the slaughter of a dear Hindu friend of mine (along with his entire family) in Chandpur, Bangladesh. I can never erase that memory from my mind. That was a devastating experience, no doubt.

More shocking was that many Muslims were happy about that and even went further to support the idea that we (Muslims) should kill more Hindus, because the Muslims in India are being slaughtered, too. It was also declared by some Muslim clerics that killing of non-Muslims is an act of *jihad* and therefore, anyone participating in *jihad* will be rewarded with Paradise. At that tender age, I knew very little about Islam and nothing about other religions. However, the little conscience inside me told me that what was being done and what was being practiced was not right. However, I had little power to change the course of events.

The other incident involves my life itself. I nearly died when the Pakistani soldiers and their fanatic supporters attacked the university residential halls on the dark night of March 25, 1971. I still do not know how I escaped the near death when most of my dear university friends were killed. There were bullets in every place. Somehow or other, I could cross the high walls; that may be impossible for me to do now. There were many other incidents during that period and just before our liberation when I escaped near death from the fanatic followers of Islam. All those incidents spawned the seed of deep religious distrust in my mind. At that time, many of my friends also shared similar views with me. And naturally, I felt very happy that we had come to the end of religious tyranny.

But alas! As strange as it may seem now, many of those dear university friends of mine have really become fanatic followers of Islam now. Many of them I met in my overseas life. They have spent a good part of their lives in the Middle East. They openly support some of the actions by the Pakistan army and their fanatical followers. They strongly support the forced conversion of the entire world's population to Islam and will do everything to bring this about. Only then, they say, "there will be peace."

Even in a country like Australia, many of these Islamists dare to say, "We came to Australia to rid the people of their sinful activities and convert them to Islam." One of their goals is to build a mosque in every suburb of Australia. Of course, these are laughing matters in a place like Australia. Whenever I meet these old pals, it really breaks my heart. When I ask them what had caused such a change in them, they readily admit that they were greatly influenced by the Arabs. Even though many of them really hate the cruel treatment (in many cases slave treatment) by the Arabs. Nevertheless, they feel very grateful to the Arabs for giving them employment and good money. Many of these Bangalis are proud to dress like Arabs. They have literally wiped out the memory of genocide in Bangladesh and some of them really justify the genocide to purify Islam. This led me to conclude that Islam is nothing but the preservation of Arab hegemony and the enslavement of the poor people of countries such as Bangladesh.

Strangely, none of these Islamists really want to migrate to any Islamic countries. None of them choose to live in an Islamic society. Why? The truth is that none of those Arab countries want them. These countries are for the Arabs only. Where is the Islamic brotherhood? The Arabs are very clever people. They have used Islam as powerful bait to continue the age-old tradition of slavery in the twenty-first century format. My guess is that this will continue escalating while the oil price keeps soaring. These fanatics use the openness and fairness of the democratic institutions in countries like Australia to propagate their poisonous doctrines.

Here are a few sentences from the Qur'an and other sources of Islam which I consider to be absolutely abhorrent, distasteful, hatemongering, and fascistic. I closely studied the Qur'an, *ahadith*, *Sharia* and *Sirah* (Mohammad's biography) before I was convinced that Islam is not a religion. Islam is false, barbaric, and imperialistic. My perception of Islam has been confirmed by the events of September 11, Madrid, Bali, Bombay, Istanbul…and so on.

> Allah made it only as glad tidings, and that your hearts be at rest therewith. And there is no victory except from Allah. Verily, Allah is All-Mighty, All-Wise. *Qur'an 8:10*

Fight against them so that Allah will punish them by your hands and disgrace them and give you victory over them and heal the breasts of a believing people, and remove the anger of their (believers') hearts. Allah accepts the repentance of whom He wills. Allah is All-Knowing, All-Wise. *Qur'an 9:14-15*

So, when you meet (in fight *jihad* in Allah's Cause), those who disbelieve smite at their necks till when you have killed and wounded many of them, then bind a bond firmly (on them, i.e. take them as captives). Thereafter (is the time) either for generosity (i.e. free them without ransom), or ransom (according to what benefits Islam), until the war lays down its burden. Thus [you are ordered by Allah to continue in carrying out *jihad* against the disbelievers till they embrace Islam (i.e. are saved from the punishment in the Hell-fire) or at least come under your protection], but if it had been Allah's Will, He Himself could certainly have punished them (without you). But (He lets you fight), in order to test you, some with others. But those who are killed in the Way of Allah, He will never let their deeds be lost. *Qur'an 47:4*

Should not the Western infidels who have fallen in love with the Islamic apologists (or the moderate, peaceful Islam) learn a few lessons from these verses? The pithy message in this verse is so loud and clear that even a primary school kid, after having diligently read those infallible words of Allah, will tell you that the perpetrators of the mayhem of 9/11, 11/3, 7/7...are simply carrying out what Allah has asked them to do. Even if 10 percent of the Muslims (this will be around 100.2 million nascent *Jihadists*) around the globe, with complete conviction in their faith, decide to act fully on these verses, this should be enough to annihilate virtually all the infidels. This is more powerful than all the atom bombs that the infidels possess. Isn't this mind-boggling?

Therefore, the simplistic logic that the vast majority of the Muslims are peace-loving, law-abiding, and not Islamic terrorists is completely void. It is not the majority of the Muslims that matters. It is that 10 percent that is the gravest concern to today's civilization. This is akin to a virus attack. I wonder why such simple and perfectly clear logic does not enter the heads of infidel politically correct politicians. They are vaguely satisfied that most Muslims are against Islamic terrorism; therefore, Islamic terrorism is bound to go away, sooner or later.

This delusion has paralyzed the Western policy makers. They believe that somehow, by resorting to politically correct politics, those utterly unchangeable verses of Allah will disappear, or at least become "not acted upon" by the overwhelming majority of Muslims. I would request these "blind" and "unenlightened" politically correct politicians visit an Islamic Paradise, and, instead of negotiating deals with the corrupt rulers, visit a mosque, a university, a college, and a *madrassa*, and inquire as to what the Muslim students believe about the meaning of *jihad* or what these people think of terror attacks on Western cities. The glib answer from this newest breed of Islamists might make these uninformed infidels quake in absolute fear. For sure, these Muslim students will provide a clear explanation of the above verses: That is, the Qur'an unmistakably calls for the complete destruction of infidels in the hands of Muslims by any means.

Let us now briefly review what the rest of the civilized world is doing to face such an implacable foe.

Here are some of the steps the infidels have adopted to assuage a "raging," seemingly unstoppable, Islamic terror:

> Guaranteeing the preaching and indoctrination of Islam through the construction of a plethora of new mosques, *madrassahs*, *mussalas*, Islamic colleges, Islamic primary schools/nurseries, Islamic universities, etc. In Islamic Paradises, proselytizing any religion other than Islam is a serious offense; it might be punishable by a death sentence;

> Allowing unabated immigration of Islamists in infidel territories, forgetting that the only reason these Islamists migrate to infidel lands is to convert these *haram/najis* (impure) lands into pure Islamic Paradises by hook or by crook, and if necessary, by colluding with the Islamic terrorists living and flourishing amidst them and in the Middle East;

> Allowing unrestricted growth of Islamic centers and Islamic student organizations in universities and colleges. These are the fertile grounds for the hidden Islamic terrorists;

> Permitting the Islamists to use valuable space in educational institutions, offices, and factories to be reserved for prayer pur-

poses. This right of prayer space (the infidels refer to this gesture as religious freedom; the Islamists laugh at the stupidity of the infidels) is not extended for other religions, or denied when requested. One might wonder why there is such a policy of duplicity. Why only the Muslim students/workers/staff members should have such privileges—even when some members of their community are hell-bent to destroy Western civilization? Is this the correct approach to combat Islamic extremism/terrorism?— by feeding these barbaric Islamists with nutrition and letting them breed unchecked?

Just to confirm that the infidels have reaped what they have been sowing for many years, on July 7, 2005, the "real Islam" struck London with crushing alacrity—Allah's unbound vengeance. Since this day in Britain's infamy they have also attempted to strike again and will continue to do so.

So, how will the British government (or other infidel governments) tackle the menace of this radical Islam? Here are some of my predictions:

Non-Muslims will be barred from visiting Islamic centers and mosques. This measure will be taken in response to the demand by the "peaceful" Islamists for more freedom to do what they would like to do at mosques and Islamic centers, so that no non-Muslim will be allowed to interfere in their affairs. The infidels call this respect for privacy.

There will be more interfaith dialogues, which mean providing the Islamists with a strong platform to severely criticize/attack Western civilization. In Islam, there is no such thing as "interfaith dialogue." Just go to an Islamic Paradise and mention these words and the Islamists will laugh at you.

It will be illegal to quote hateful verses from the Qur'an and *Hadis*.

Web sites analyzing and dissecting Islam will be ordered to close down. However, the infidel government will subsidize Islamic organizations to set up and maintain Islamic websites to preach "peaceful," "moderate" Islam. In infidels' language, this is called an "outreach" program.

Anyone who utters any word, sentence, or message, or anyone who demonstrates his/her misdemeanor towards Islam/Muslims, or whose words offend any Islamist, will face a hefty fine or court action (similar to a traffic offense).

Anyone who discusses Islamic terrorism and surreptitiously squints at any Muslim that happens to be nearby will be arrested and fined. The infidels call this a "vilification" act. However, Muslims will be allowed to criticize Christianity, Judaism, Buddhism, Hinduism.

Mosques will be allowed to use loudspeakers to spread, five times a day, the beautiful, melodious cry of Islam. After all, for a long time the Muslims (living in infidel lands) have complained that the denial of such opportunity had always been a sore point. They have always complained about their lack of religious freedom to inseminate the environmentally friendly, clear, silent air with heavenly cheers (read Azan). For other religions, though, using loudspeakers outside their enclosed congregation hall will be treated as an unbearable noise pollution. The organizers of such religious functions will be charged with disturbing the peace. Islam's prayer noise will be treated as divine music.

Any newspaper that publishes articles that Islamists render as offensive to Islam will face severe punitive measures. Government rulings will force the infidel newspapers to provide free advertising space to spread peaceful Islam (refer to the Australian case). Islamists will be able to publish articles defaming other religions. This is known as Islamic tolerance, and the un-Islamic, infidel governments will respect this brand of Islamic tolerance.

To placate the Islamists, infidel governments will accede to their demand for *Sharia* laws to be applied to the Muslims. Muslims will have their own parliament—the Islamic *Majlis* or *Shura* council. Muslims will have their separate "Ministry" and "Judiciary." They will even have separate beaches, playgrounds, gymnasiums, fitness centers, picnic spots, ablution centers, baby care centers, hostels, maternity clinics, public toilets, restaurants, aged care facilities, markets (only *halal* stuff), hospitals... Any bikini-clad or un-Islamically dressed woman found in an Islamic beach or other Islamic spots will face an Islamic *Sharia* court. Since she was in an Islamic territory, she will be subject to Islamic laws; the secular laws prevalent for the vast majority of infidels will not apply to her.

When meeting a Muslim man, an infidel woman must be attired in *hijab* and/or black cassock to respect Islam. No handshake will be allowed. This procedure will become a law. Any infidel woman breaking this provision will be tried in a *Sharia* court and not in a secular court.

In universities and colleges, if there is even a single Muslim/Muslimah, any student who talks about Islam will be subject to disciplinary action. The lecturer/professor/teacher must allow the Muslim student to enter and leave the class as he/she deems necessary to perform *Salat* (prayer). Special assessment procedures will apply to Muslim students—to uphold the affirmative action policy. This will compensate for the past historical discrimination and injustice perpetrated by the colonists.

The British government will accede to the demand of the Islamists for training in self-defense, to protect them from the despicable skinheads. Muslims will be allowed to form their own defense or vigilante corps. In the future, this Islamic defense corps will demand a certain territory within Great Britain to be exclusively reserved for the Muslims. Unbelievably, the British government will satisfy this Islamic demand.

The readers might laugh at some of my imaginary ideas, which are especially applicable to the Islamists living in infidel lands. But wait a minute; this is exactly what the Qur'an says. Muslims are Allah's exceptional creation. The infidel world owes them a living, otherwise they are allowed by Allah to create terror, destruction, and mayhem. They deserve those extraordinary treatments because Allah says they are destined to rule the world and subdue all other religions.

What happens if the infidels refuse to accord those special privileges to the Islamists? The answer is the verse quoted above: you get 9/11, 3/11, 7/7, Bali, Jakarta, Casablanca, Istanbul...

When the world's best intelligence organizations, such as the CIA, FBI, Scotland Yard, MI5, MI6, etc. fail to trace a single clue as to who these mindless terrorists are (before their attacks), and why they are perpetrating such heinous acts, one wonders what is wrong with these reputed establishments? The answer to this enigma is very easy. These infidels do not understand Islam. They are only fishing in the wrong water. They think Islamic terrorists are like the IRA, Tamil Tigers, Basque separatists, Communist terrorists, etc. They are utterly wrong. To fight Islamic terrorists they must understand Islam first. Before they pick up any surveillance tool, they must pick up the Qur'an and read it thoroughly. Before they train on any weapon, they must read the *Hadis* and *Sharia* and see their "beauty."

This is exactly how the Islamists train their *Jihadists*. They (the Islamist terrorists) are indoctrinated first in "real Islam" before they learn how to handle explosives and the use of arms and ammunitions. They know exactly how to imbue the Islamic fighters. The infidels are just callous; they put the cart before the horse. Don't you think the Islamists are smarter than all those world-famous intelligence organizations? Let us face the truth: in strategic planning, cunningness, and smarts these Islamists simply beat the infidels' intelligence teams hands down.

Therefore, the anti-terrorist squads (of infidels) must learn a few lessons from the Islamists. They should learn how to beat their enemy in their own game. Once these squads learn what real Islam is all about, it will be so simple to map out the correct strategies to extinguish Islamic terrorism—for good. Moreover, it costs so little to know "real Islam"!

A good starting point will be to comprehend the above verses. An old adage says, "Know your enemy." This is true, but, the truer version should be, "Know your enemy's motive." The motive of the Islamists is Islam—not terrorism, not Iraq, not Afghanistan. Terrorism is just a tool employed, but the Qur'an is the motivator, and Islam is the final goal. There can be no clearer message than this. The civilized world is at war—a war with Islam. The Islamists will surely confirm this truth.

Ignore the above immutable words of Allah (the Qur'anic verses quoted above), and the defeat of the infidels is guaranteed.

CHAPTER SEVENTEEN

WE NEED TO STICK TOGETHER

"I would disagree that I'm safe to practice my faith (or 'nonbelief') in a Western democracy. Unfortunately, it looks more like a dhimmicracy *to me each day."*

WHILE MANY PEOPLE believe the violent strain within Islam is not representative of the entire religion, others challenge the West to read the sacred texts of Islam and to see how and why these fundamentalists may be interpreting the Qur'an correctly. Furthermore, many people who have left Islam believe the only way forward is for the world to unite and begin to truly appreciate the freedoms we enjoy and do everything we can to maintain them. This letter reminds us that the freedoms we enjoy are worth living and fighting for. Basharee Mortadd fears that Westerners don't know Islam like he does. His story shows what's wrong with Islam and why it's not right for the West.

Basharee Mortadd's Testimony

I was born to Muslim parents who, like most religious parents, were guilty of indoctrinating their children into a religion they never even chose for themselves. Fortunately for me, I always kept an open mind. I was also smart enough to keep my mouth shut until I moved to a Western country. Soon after, I learned enough about Islam to have had enough of it. I felt so ashamed to even feel proud of this ideology of hate. I cannot believe I used to actually invite non-Muslims to this faith. But my intentions were not evil. I used to invite them because they were my friends (being the ignorant Muslim I was, I did not let the fact that I cannot befriend non-Muslims sink into my head). I did not want them to go to hell because I loved them and I wanted to "save" them from an eternal punishment.

I am glad they were not interested in my invitations and preaching. Westerners today tend to be so anti-Christian they want to turn to any other faith. Being a simplistic (read: primitive) religion and properly sanitized by deceiving Muslims, they find it appealing to convert to Islam. You particularly find that among non-white people who want to rebel against what they perceive to be an exclusively white religion.

Being an ex-Muslim, one would expect that I have been liberated and that I am living in happiness. You expect me to move on with my life and to put my past life of darkness and ignorance behind.

I truly wish that were the case. Don't take me wrong. I have never felt more liberated than during the first days during which I felt I no longer feared the fictitious Allah. It's an amazing feeling to realize that you can think for yourself, and be your own prophet. In fact, allow me to sound boastful when I say that leaving Islam is a powerful intellectual accomplishment. People who have not lived in *Dar Al-Islam* cannot and will not understand the level of indoctrination Muslims undergo for their entire lives. When you don't train your muscles, you become physically weak. It's no different with the mind. If you've never used your mind but rather simply lived under the culture of submission ("Islam" means "submission," by the way), your ability to think withers.

Submission to whom? To your parents, to your teachers, to your local *imam*, to your king. Dare not question. Dare not think differently from the majority or you will face ostracism at best and death at worst. (Personally, I would prefer getting killed instead of facing humiliation from a community.)

Yet it is far from over. Being an ex-Muslim is just the beginning. When Neo swallowed the red pill, the movie did not end and we had two (poorly scripted) sequels of *The Matrix*.

The reasons I still seem attached to Islam are numerous. To name a few:

First off, I have to live as a closet apostate. The founder of Islam gave me good reasons fourteen hundred years ago:

> Sahih Bukhari, Volume 9, Book 83, Number 17: The blood of a Muslim who confesses that none has the right to be worshipped but Allah and that I am His Apostle, cannot be shed except in three cases: In *Qisas* for murder, a married person who commits illegal sexual intercourse and the one who reverts from Islam (apostate) and leaves the Muslims. (Repeated in Sahih Muslim.)

> Sahih Bukhari, Volume 9, Book 84, Number 57: Whoever changed his Islamic religion, then kill him. (Repeated here.)

> Sahih Bukhari, Volume 9, Book 84, Number 58: There was a fettered man beside Abu Muisa. Mu'adh asked, "Who is this (man)?" Abu Muisa said, "He was a Jew and became a Muslim and then reverted back to Judaism." Then Abu Muisa requested Mu'adh to sit down but Mu'adh said, "I will not sit down till he has been killed. This is the judgment of Allah and His Apostle (for such cases) and repeated it thrice. Then Abu Musa ordered that the man be killed, and he was killed. (Repeated here, and in Sahih Muslim as well.)

Phew. *Argumentum ad baculum* is definitely not a convincing argument for me to return to Islam, but this seventh-century madman sure did give me good reason to keep my apostasy to myself. I hate it. It seems that I can see the light and the world outside this cage but I still cannot go out and enjoy what life has to give. I still have to pretend I'm a Muslim. I am never at ease with myself when I'm not being myself. I was never a good liar (and that's a blessing).

I would disagree that I'm safe to practice my faith (or "nonbelief") in a Western democracy. Unfortunately, it looks more like a *dhimmicracy* to me each day. It frustrates me how the West tries to appease those who hate us and want us converted, subjugated, or killed (I'm looking at you, CAIR).

I want to save the product of Judeo-Christian reform called the West. Many of those born into the West do not appreciate what it means to be born with free will, with guaranteed free speech, and with a separation of the church and state. Coming from the hellhole of Islam, I do, and I intend to preserve it. I will not allow my children to go through the psychological hell Islamic nations are going through. I will not allow it for your children.

Islam is a dangerous political ideology that separates the world into "us" versus "them," into Muslim versus *kafir*, into *Dar Al-Islam* versus *Dar Al-Harb*. If there is anything I want you to learn from this boring rant, it's this: Muslims cannot coexist in peace with non-Muslims. Muslims hate you and will never be pleased with you unless you're a living Muslim, a humiliated *dhimmi*, or a dead infidel:

> Fight those who do not believe in Allah, nor in the latter day, nor do they prohibit what Allah and His Messenger have prohibited, nor follow the religion of truth, out of those who have been given the Book, until they pay the tax in acknowledgment of superiority and they are in a state of subjection. *Qur'an 9:29*

When we talk about tolerance, we mean one of two things: Either that Islam will be peaceful only when the whole world becomes Muslim, or that we are tolerant enough to allow Jews, Christians, and Zoroastrians to live among us as second-class citizens under the *dhimma* treaty.

I want to help my people. They are infected with the illness of Islam and I wish to save them from it. Unfortunately, I need to set my feelings aside and realize that it is unlikely to result in mass apostasy. Educating them into being human beings is slow compared to their high procreation rates, which was also ordered by their Prophet.

The West must, then, learn the truth about Islam so we can ban Muslim immigration and figure out how to handle the Muslim populations already living among us (well, near us—they usually live in ghettos and in closed circles).

Generally, I have been trying to help in other ways that I shall not disclose for obvious safety reasons. However, I have noticed the growth of apostate bloggers lately, and that got me thinking of having a blog for myself in support of those brave brethren. We need to stand together during this difficult time. What better place to do it than on the Internet and in the blogosphere, where the worst that can happen to us is to receive hate mail and death threats? Thanks to the Internet, the truth will be shown. Muslims can no longer harm us because we use anonymous identities.

I urge all apostates of Islam to open up Web sites and blogs exposing the truth about Islam. In fact, you need not even write about Islam in your blog. Just mention that you are an apostate and write about anything else, be it your job, your dog, your obsession with Ann Coulter (off the top of my head), et cetera. Merely mentioning your apostasy is sufficient to sow the seeds of doubt in Muslims who find apostasy to be as impossible as dividing a number by zero.

Let us stand in solidarity with these fine soldiers!

> And say: The truth has come and the falsehood has vanished; surely falsehood is a vanishing (thing). *Qur'an 17:81*

> وَقُلْ جَاءَ الْحَقُّ وَزَهَقَ الْبَاطِلُ إِنَّ الْبَاطِلَ كَانَ زَهُوقًا

CHAPTER EIGHTEEN

I MISSED A PRAYER AND DIDN'T TURN TO STONE

"When I was about ten years old, my father started hauling me along to the annual rites commemorating the seventh-century beheading of Imam Ali's son Hussein. At first, I was allowed to simply slap my chest during the processions, but by the time I was twelve, I'd graduated to flogging myself with chains."

WHILE THE TITLE of this chapter might sound preposterous, such is the level of indoctrination within Islam that Esfahani believed it. Time and time again we hear of indoctrination within Islam that breeds hatred and fear towards any other mindset, including freedom. Today, Esfahani is an apostate yet still has the dilemma of raising his children without faith. Indeed, for many who leave Islam, it is not just a matter of no longer attending Friday prayer but a total change in their complete way of life. Consequently, those who say goodbye are sometimes left isolated, rejected, and confused. Who can they turn to for support, not only for themselves but also for their families? It is this sad reality that makes these stories all the more compelling.

Esfahani's message is simple: Far better to raise a family outside of Islam than within it. He is glad he left Islam, and he urges Westerners to look hard at the dangers that come from the religion.

Esfahani's Testimony

I am a forty-seven-year-old man, married with two teen children. I am originally from Esfahan. My city of origin, Esfahan, is considered one of the most religious cities in Iran. Esfahanis, in general, have been a source of reliance for the Islamic regime of Iran. My city of birth is notorious as the "number one" supplier of martyrs, intelligence agents, torturers, jailers, *mullahs*, and occasionally religious scholars, politicians, and intellectuals since the 1979 revolution. I grew up in such a religious environment in a very typical religious Esfahani family.

I was born in October 1961. I was the third of my parents' five children. Like most Iranians, we were Shias. We weren't zealots, but we were one of the more devout families in my neighborhood. My parents' piety was, for me, the most salient feature of my childhood.

My father made sure that his children performed their daily prayers, and as we got older he saw to it that we observed the fasts of Ramadan. When I was about ten years old, my father started hauling me along to the annual rites commemorating the seventh-century beheading of Imam Ali's son Hussein. At first, I was allowed to simply slap my chest during the processions, but by the time I was twelve, I'd graduated to flogging myself with chains. A few years later, when I was in high school, I often found myself alone in the school mosque during the noontime prayer. This was the atmosphere in which I spent most of my teen years.

By the late 1970s, dissatisfaction with the Shah was becoming universal. Many Iranians began to openly express their opposition to the Shah and their support for Khomeini. As this wave of opposition swept over Esfahan, I joined the Revolution. At first, I participated in the actions of groups who opposed the Shah for religious reasons. These groups orchestrated the closing of Esfahan's schools and prodded businesses in the city's bazaars to shut down to demonstrate their solidarity. I also joined mobs that vandalized banks and other institutions on which the regime depended.

In the fall of 1978, I had a chance encounter with an older cousin. My cousin was also dedicated to the overthrow of the Shah, but he belonged to a socialist group whose vision for Iran's future was quite unlike that pictured by the religious right. We had a long discussion about the Revolution. I remember our conversation and my cousin's scorn for my religious views.

When my cousin explained his own nonreligious reasons for opposing the Shah, I felt ashamed and foolish. That very day, I made the decision to neglect my evening prayers. As I fell asleep that night, I thought it unlikely that I'd wake the next morning. I expected—as my parents had raised me to expect—that I would be turned to stone. When I woke up, flesh and blood, the next morning, I abandoned Islam! To this day, after almost thirty years of passage of time, I still feel ambivalent about the suddenness of this transformation. Nevertheless, the change must have been rooted firmly, as I have never been tempted to return to the fold.

How we overthrew the Shah of Iran, what I experienced as a soldier serving in the Iranian army in Mehran during the Iran/Iraq war, how I eventually escaped across the border into Pakistan, taking then a U-turn towards the West all the way into Mexico and across the Rio Grande River into the U.S.A., are all stories unrelated to what has caused me to write to you today. What I have mentioned to you so far is just an overview of what I stand for today and how I got to it.

Today, I have two children. My goal is to be a father who deserves respect and provides guidance. My children often confront me with questions I have a hard time responding to. Before I made a decision to become a father, I thought it would be wise to teach my children to be humans with love, respect, and tolerance for all. My mind was set to raise them free from the tight grasp of all religions with a mind not limited by the threat of the all-mighty God. What I had failed to anticipate was the reality of what our society is made of and how others' culture and beliefs affect us.

How am I supposed to respond when my children come from school wondering why their classmates have stories about their weekend experience at Senegal, Church, Mosque, and Temple to share with each other while my children don't even know what these places are for? How do I respond when they ask me, referring to the Muslims' Ramadan, the Christians' Christmas, and the Jews' Yom Kippur: "Daddy when or what do we celebrate?" How do I explain what "In God We Trust" embroiled on all our monetary notes means? In sum, how do I free my family from the grasp of religion while the Constitution only guarantees the freedom of religion?

CHAPTER NINETEEN

BORN INTO ISLAM, RAISED IN THE U.S.

"President Bush and others are dead wrong when they say that Islam is a great and peaceful faith that has been hijacked by a few extremists. In fact, Islam is a vile and violent faith that establishes extremism..."

MANY PEOPLE have suggested that the violent strain within Islam is inspired through a literal interpretation of the Qur'an. However, some former Muslims contend that this violent strain is in fact the truest expression of Islam. It is interesting to note that this testimony does not come from the Middle East or an Islamic nation but here in the United States, a place where they feel free to question the notion that Islam is a religion of peace.

This letter urges all of us to realize that Islam is part of the problem, not the solution. Only by acknowledging what it stands for can we successfully stand against it. And if we don't stand against it, we in the West will find ourselves under its oppressive power.

Testimony of an Apostate who Found Freedom in the U.S.

I was born in an Islamic country to Muslim parents, but I was raised in the United States. Throughout my life, I considered myself to be a Muslim, and I maintained a large arsenal of uninformed apologies, explanations, and blind denials to promote and defend Islam. Of course, I had never once read the Qur'an, and I had relied exclusively on what I heard from my parents, my relatives, my Muslim friends, and the Islamic media.

Then one day, at the age of twenty-six, I decided to read the Qur'an so that I could become a "better Muslim." The first three pages alone shocked me with their illogic and obvious contradictions with the constant claim that Allah was the "most merciful" and "most compassionate," but I closed my eyes, gritted my teeth, held on tightly, and pushed ahead with absolute certainty that it would all be explained and would get better. However, it only got worse—much worse.

After reading the Qur'an, I realized that I couldn't possibly endorse Islam as a religion, as a philosophy, as a moral standard, as an ethical code, or even as useful fiction. I determined that these philosophies and this image of Allah could only come from an extremely warped and disturbed person who suffered from an aggregation of the most severe and profound human weaknesses.

Since 1996, I've read and re-read the Qur'an and the *Hadiths* (which are even worse than the Qur'an), and I've always reached the same conclusion—Islam is an absolute disaster for the entire world, for Christians, for Jews, for pagans, for atheists, for women, for children, and, most of all, for Muslims themselves.

I've discussed Islam's fundamental weaknesses endlessly with many relatives and friends, and nobody has ever been able to respond in any meaningful way. Nobody has ever been able to manufacture any legitimate story that indicates that Islam is a useful or positive force on this earth. From the Islamic apologists, I hear that somehow the Jews are responsible for my betrayal. I hear that I've been "brainwashed" by the media, which, according to them, is Jewish. I hear that I need to understand Islamic "history" to understand the unlimited illogic, cruelty, internal inconsistency, and injustice. I hear that somebody, somewhere in some distant Islamic country, could validly answer my questions, but the people I speak with can say only that there is some good explanation, but that they don't know enough to tell me.

Of course, when those allegedly wise Muslims appear, they themselves can't possibly answer the questions and they play the same game—it's the Jews, it's the media, I don't know enough Islamic history to understand, and they know somebody eight thousand miles away who could explain it all to me. Ultimately, nobody can sufficiently explain how the Qur'an is anything other than arbitrary, cruel, unjust, evil, and riddled with evidence that it is based on the most profound human weaknesses. I don't use those terms lightly or imprecisely or emotionally. As a matter of dispassionate fact, Islam—as written in the Qur'an—is arbitrary, cruel, unjust, and evil, and it contains endless conclusive evidence that the founder of this "religion" suffered from the most intense form of the worst human weaknesses on earth.

Of course, my life has improved drastically since I read the Qur'an and realized the obvious human weaknesses from which it originated. I sincerely hope that all Muslims will read the Qur'an and simply think about whether this religion comes from a good person or a bad person, from an intelligent person or from a fool, from good or from evil, from compassion or from cruelty, from justice or injustice, from decency or from depravity— however anyone wants to define those terms.

Islam is, in fact, the problem for the entire world, but the biggest problem on earth for Muslims themselves. Unfortunately, in addition to destroying themselves with Islam, the rest of the world is likely to meet its end as soon as true Muslims assemble the weaponry required to destroy the earth.

It's absolutely imperative that the people who I call "pretend Muslims"—who are the vast majority of people who call themselves Muslims—disassociate themselves from this bizarre superstition called Islam and from the few true believers who rely on the pretend Muslims for their strength and legitimacy. President Bush and others are dead wrong when they say that Islam is a great and peaceful faith that has been hijacked by a few extremists. In fact, Islam is a vile and violent faith that establishes extremism and that has been hijacked by the pretend Muslims who, by their own human decency, have given this barbaric superstition the appearance of legitimacy to the uninformed.

CHAPTER TWENTY

MY LEAVING ISLAM TESTIMONY

"[After leaving Islam], I am starting college. I choose what I want to wear, I choose how I want to live. I am bringing my kids up away from the damaging effects of Islam. I hope more Muslims than ever leave Islam this year and the next and the next until none are left."

WHILE TERROR ATTACKS have traumatized the world, some apostates have experienced their own form of terrorism and persecution within their own homes. In Shara's story we learn how persecution and tyranny within Islamic families is tolerated and can find itself in a family home in England. Indeed, in recent years we have witnessed the term and seen the effects of "honor killing" in many western cities. Shara's testimony gives even more evidence that women frequently suffer under Islam—even in the West.

Shara's Testimony

My father, who is Moroccan, came over to England in the early '70s. He applied on a student visa at the time, and immigration was a good thing rather than what it has become today.

He wasn't a strict Muslim at the time; he was quite a rebel. He met my mother, who was English, not long after he came over. And after seeing her a few times, he decided to marry her.

She was sixteen when she married my father, still not aware of Muslims and the truth. After about a year of marriage, my sister was born; things were not good between my parents. He was violent and would lash out at my mother quite often, and most of the time over silly things like too much salt in the food, etc.

He was obviously trying to push her into being a good Muslim woman, and her loving him meant that she stayed and gave birth to me two years after my sister, and then gave birth to my younger sister another four years later.

As a Muslim man, my father grew angry at the fact that my mother had only given birth to three girls. He beat my mother very badly; she was hospitalized and the doctors were forced to remove her womb from where he had beaten her so badly. It was the only way to save her life. When she awoke, my father was kind enough to tell her that he would be divorcing her now that she could no longer have children, and being a man, he needed a son.

She ran away from him and she ran away from us. When my younger sister was only six months old, my mother packed her stuff and left our life for good; we never saw her again until I was twenty years old (but that is a whole other story). I was only four years old at the time, and was not old enough to understand why she had left us. All I could see was that she couldn't have loved us.

My father couldn't cope with three kids, so he gave us up, and placed us in a children's home. It was a temporary thing, until he could get himself sorted out. It took him three years. He used to visit us while we were living there.

Can you imagine how lost and alone we all felt; one second we had a mum, she left, and the next day my dad gave us away? Needless to say I was a very screwed up young girl.

But I look back on the three years we had in that children's home with a certain fondness, because that was the only time in my life when I experienced the fun of being a child. When I turned seven, my father came back for us and took us to his house to live. But first he needed to get married, so off we all went to Morocco for his arranged wedding.

Our family over there was taking no chances on him marrying a *kafir* woman again, and had handpicked a lady from the village.

We met her, and she seemed nice enough. We were desperate for a mother's love.

My father married this lady and we returned to England to start our family life. Things went bad right away: My father became religious and my stepmother was a monster. She had barely been in the country for a few months when we first experienced a physical beating.

Because we had lived in an English home before my father took us back, we couldn't speak Moroccan, so the first thing my parents implemented was a new rule. No speaking in the house unless it was in Moroccan. Seeing how we didn't know any of it, and we were talkative kids, we broke the rule. My sister said "Dad" instead of the Moroccan equivalent. She was whipped across her back until she bled; we all were as they felt that all should be punished whenever any one of us broke a rule.

Life changed quickly, and my childhood was spent in a haze of pain, beatings, and tears. Amongst the various physical punishments were whippings, burnings (where a red hot knife would be placed on our skin), being tied up and left there, and being force-fed excrement. I do not lie, these are the things they did to train us, but I wouldn't even train a dog like that.

We were taught the Qur'an, and how to recite it; any mistakes and we were beaten. We did all the chores, and we covered ourselves when at school. We were not allowed to have friends, and we never went anywhere. The only times we ever had fun was when we were on holiday in Morocco. Then our parents were too busy to notice us most of the time.

Later, I was eleven and on holiday in Morocco. My father beat me badly in the *medina* (a place in town where everybody goes); he was very cruel. That was the first time I tried to kill myself. I just wanted to die, to give up, and I took as many pills as I could find and I swallowed them. Sadly all I did was make myself very ill. I spent the whole night puking, and my uncle was really worried; he ran and fetched my dad, who took one look at me lying there and said, "Good, let her die." Believe me, at that moment all I wanted to do was die.

I didn't die; I carried on. We came back to England, and life carried on the same: beatings and crying late at night.

One day when I was thirteen, my stepmother went too far while beating me. I returned home late from school (not very late) because I had been studying in the library. I walked in to the house and she just jumped on me. She had a ladies high heel shoe, and used the heel part to beat me on the head. She just kept hitting and hitting. I remember feeling something warm running down my face. I remember putting my hands over my face and pulling them away to see that they were both covered with blood, so much blood.

I passed out. When I woke up in the hospital, they told me that I had been in a coma for three months.

Academically, I was a top student. I passed all my exams on a regular basis and I was about to be awarded with the first sponsorship from my school to go to NASA when I was sixteen. These were all dreams because my father never would have let me go. Here is an example of his attitude about learning: I loved to read, so I would sneak books up to my room and read them whenever I got a spare moment. My book collection became a bit too hard to hide and my father discovered my books. He beat me and made me watch while he burned them; he then placed the Qur'an in my hand and said that was the only book I should be reading.

But my stepmother's attack on my skull and the subsequent three-month coma set me back. I was never able to fully recover. Where once numbers made sense and science was as easy as riding a bike, all I could see was confusion. I became stupid.

I was placed into a state-funded home, because my parents no longer had the right to care for me. I just kind of drifted about pointlessly. I quit school, ashamed at how low my grades had become in some classes. People knew what had happened to me, but I was too ashamed to face them.

When I was seventeen, I went on holiday with my family, to Morocco. I knew how bad my parents had been to me, and I no longer lived at home, but I still craved family love, so I gave them this chance and went away with them. I knew the risks. I packed away copies of my passport and birth certificate, some extra money, and the contact details for the British embassy over there. I was worried that they would try to keep me over there by force.

That shouldn't have been my only worry. I didn't wear a *hijab* at this stage, and dressed how I wanted to. I was raped on that holiday by a cousin; when he had finished the deed he looked at me and said that I couldn't tell anyone because no one would believe me, and the way I had been dressed meant people wouldn't blame him.

I knew he was right. I cried myself to sleep the whole time I was there. No one understood why I became a recluse, or why I made my uncle escort me everywhere—even my uncle didn't know. I just needed a chaperone.

What's worse is that a few years later I told my sister what had happened. I needed to tell someone; I needed someone to tell me it wasn't my fault. She went and told my parents. They didn't believe me. My father shouted at me, and my stepmother told me to consider myself lucky as he was a fine young man.

Nothing hurt as much as that... at least not yet.

I spent seven years doing what I wanted, going where I wanted. Wearing what I wanted. But I was still a Muslim at heart. I just considered myself to be a non-practicing Muslim. I had issues, and even though my father was so cruel to me, I still tried to gain his admiration and acceptance.

I met my ex-husband when I was twenty. I was at a petrol station and we just started talking. He seemed so nice and polite, and had a nice smile. He was also a Moroccan, which was perfect because I still wanted my dad to love me. He asked me out on a date, and I accepted. We had a good time, and continued to see each other when I had time off from work.

He told me he was working (I later found out this was a lie). He used to lay my head in his lap, and stroke my hair; he was affectionate and considerate. I was swept up. For someone who felt as unloved as I had all my life, I finally thought that I had found it.

Those first six months between us were so special. I treasure those memories even though it hurts to do so.

We got married, and I became pregnant when I was twenty-one. That was when I found out who my husband really was.

Where once he had greeted me with kindness, now insults would spew from his mouth at all hours of the day. Where once he used to be affectionate, he now mocked me, and told me that someone like me didn't deserve love. Where we used to enjoy nights out at the cinema, or a restaurant, now I was not allowed anywhere, and he wasn't interested in, as he put it, "Western baloney."

The first time he hit me, it was just a slap. I say just a slap because I grew up with abuse so I could kind of look past it.

I had my own home at the time, not owned by me, but provided for me by the council. It was small but it was home, and he used to live there with me.

The abuse just got worse. He would call me names for not wearing a *hijab*, so I put one on to make him stop. Still he didn't stop. He got worse: He started to kick me, strangle me, and punch me.

When I was eight months pregnant with our first child, he came home angry one day. I opened the door to greet him and he kicked me right through our double doors. It didn't matter that I was pregnant to him; he kicked me in my stomach with no regard for his son that I was carrying.

I sadly just felt that I deserved it all. Is it any wonder that I felt it was okay to be treated this way, that this was all I was worth?

Also, Islamically I felt obliged to keep on trying, to bear with it. I gave birth, but nothing got better. I still stayed with him, though. I had no control over my own life; he would not allow me to listen to music, to watch TV, to read my books. (I love to read—books are my passion and my escape.)

I wasn't allowed to see my friends anymore. I became housebound as he felt that because I was half English I was more likely to be unfaithful.

Whenever he beat me, he would always say that he was allowed to; this is why I get so angry when Muslims try to say that that verse is there to be a deterrent. It is permission to beat your wife from God.

I won't bore you with a long in-depth look into the whole eight years that I spent with him, but I will pick out a few moments to highlight.

The day the Twin Towers went down, he was so happy. He was celebrating the death of all those people; his mother held a big party and many Muslims came to her house to celebrate. I had to sit there and watch them replay the attack over and over again. I was furious inside. He could see how much I hated him for liking death. When we got home he punished me suitably and called me a Jew lover.

This man did some awful things to me when I was married to him. He tried to run me over with his car, and threw me out of a moving car. He beat me in front of my sons.

He would tell me all the time how beneath him I was because I was not a pure Muslim, just half. I tried so hard to please him; I threw myself into the religion and tried to prove myself worthy. But nothing I did was ever good enough. I prayed to Allah to save me, but there is no Allah, so no one replied.

When I found out I was pregnant with a girl, I knew it was time to leave. I didn't want my daughter to grow up thinking she was worth less than a man, or thinking that it's okay for a man to hit a woman. I didn't want her to be ashamed of me.

As her mother I am her role model. What kind of role model would I have been if I had stayed with him?

So I packed my stuff one day when he was out, and I ran away. I took my kids with me (unlike my real mother).

This day I will always remember until the day I die. I stopped a taxi, and we all got into it. I left him and I was so pleased. I took off my *hijab* when we were a safe distance from the house, and I threw it out of the taxi window. You should have seen the look on the driver's face; he was shocked to say the least.

I let my ex-husband have contact with the kids for a while, but I have now stopped that, as he is teaching them the usual Islamic lies, and the kids are becoming harder to handle.

Truly though, my freedom only began when I found Faith Freedom International (FFI), an organization that assists former Muslims who wish to leave the faith. FFI opened my eyes to a whole new way of looking at life. And now I am hopeful that things can only get better from here on out. It is not easy moving past all the brainwashing that we ex-Muslims have gone through as children. I still judge myself and I still find moments where I wonder if I am doing the right thing, but then I only have to pick up the Qur'an to remember and I feel even better. One day I won't even have those moments anymore.

I am starting college. I choose what I want to wear, I choose how I want to live. I am bringing my kids up away from the damaging effects of Islam. I hope more Muslims than ever leave Islam this year and the next and the next until none are left.

CHAPTER TWENTY-ONE

ESCAPE FROM TURKEY

"After I had converted [to Islam]... I learned that I could be beaten by my husband, if he wasn't satisfied with me. But in my addled mind I tried to find justification for that commandment. Moreover, I was sure that my husband was incapable of hitting a woman."

W HILE INTELLIGENCE AGENCIES become more profi- cient in tracking terrorists, it is important to bear in mind that terror organizations will also become more resourceful in acquiring converts. Indeed, in the years ahead, converts to the fundamentalist strain of Islam will not fit the traditional profile of an Islamic terrorist and will be able to slip through undetected by government agencies. Furthermore, with increasing Islamic birth rates there will be far more conversions to Islam. In light of this it is important to know what conversion meant for Jutta in her na- tive country of Germany.

Jutta's Testimony

I was born to a very pious Catholic family in Berlin. Nothing pres- aged that I would become a Muslim one day; in fact, to the con- trary, everyone expected me to be a faithful Catholic throughout my life and pass down my faith to my children.

However, I had a very rebellious character and, like many adolescents, abominated everything my parents liked. I set a goal for myself to find a liberating religion different from that of my parents. I was convinced that nothing could be worse than Chris- tianity with its oppressive teachings on women.

The religious atmosphere in my family was getting on my nerves. I was having heated arguments with my parents all the time because of my disagreement with some Christian teachings. They pressed me to be a better Christian; I rebelled and did the opposite.

Soon after my graduation from university, I met a young Muslim man of Turkish origin. We fell in love and soon got married. He was not a religious fanatic—he was absolutely secular, although he did observe some Islamic obligations (he fasted and prayed). He didn't ask me to convert to his religion but he made it clear that he would like his children to be Muslims. I myself took great interest in his religion and customs. I expressed willingness to learn more about Islam.

He brought me some deceptive (as I now understand) books about the glory of Islam and benefits of being a Muslim woman. I read the books and grasped the "beauty" of this religion.

I was taught by my Christian parents that a woman had to submit to her husband and thus find God. My Muslim husband seemed to be so close to God without any help from priests and I was told that I didn't have to get married and submit to my husband to find peace of mind and faith in God. I looked at my husband and blindly believed all those lies because he was such a nice man who was the living example of a decent Muslim man. When I prayed behind him, I felt I was getting closer to God and Heaven.

Looking back on those days, I see that I was just a stupid kid who drummed into herself that Islam was an ideal religion for all humankind. Perhaps I simply wanted to vex my pious parents, whom I considered to be repressive monsters.

After I had converted, I was given some other books that were not as wonderful as the previous ones. I learned that I could be beaten by my husband if he wasn't satisfied with me. But in my addled mind I tried to find justification for that commandment. Moreover, I was sure that my husband was incapable of hitting a woman.

I gave birth to our children, who were sent to a kind of kindergarten for Muslim children. I kept on working and didn't want to give up my job. My husband supported me and told me that Islam encouraged women to work and have their own lives. I can't understand how I could believe such downright lies.

A few years later he decided to perform *Hajj*. I was very excited and proud of him because, in fact, I was much more religious than my secular husband.

When he came back, I couldn't recognize him. His behavior changed dramatically and he was no longer secular. I didn't like wearing a veil and usually put it on only when I went to mosque. Now my husband told me that I had to wear a veil outside all the time. When I opened my mouth to object to his horrible behavior, he hit me in the face and told me to shut up. I was forced to quit my job and become a housewife.

He brought some books from Saudi Arabia which "reformed" him and saved him from "perishing in Hell." I read those books on Islam, the real Islam that my husband started to practice. Suddenly the scales fell from my eyes and I realized that I had never been a Muslim. But it was too late, as we were moving to Turkey. He feared that Germany would have an adverse effect on our children's upbringing.

My life in rural Turkey, with his parents, was a nightmare. I was no longer a liberated Muslimah, a wife of a liberal Muslim; I was a real Muslimah, just a commodity of my husband.

I used to enjoy praying but now I started to detest prayers led by my husband. I no longer felt close to God. When I finished reading a real, not spurious, biography of the Prophet, I felt sick. I had been lied to all the time. How could I believe that Mohammad was the prophet of God?

I wondered what had happened to my husband. He told me he had had conversations with fellow Muslims from "moral" countries like Saudi Arabia and they had opened his eyes. I put the blame for my husband's change of behavior on them, but then it occurred to me that he had always been a Muslim, although a secular one. What could I possibly expect from him? I had read dozens of articles about women married to Muslims and their hardship. I had been warned by my best friends that I was playing with fire. However, my unreasonable hatred for Christianity, my love for my husband, and the blatant lies deceived me and made me immune to reason and logic.

After such a rude awakening to the horrors of Islam and its treatment of women, I decided to review the Qur'an. My first feeling was anger at my blindness to reality. It is apparent from the Qur'an that men are given total control over women. "The Holy Book" abounds with discriminatory teachings on women, which are quite obvious from the context of the book. Only a blind woman in love like me could overlook them.

When my husband realized that I was no longer a docile wife and a pious Muslimah, he became a real savage. He showed his true colors and exclaimed that German whores could never become modest women.

Even his ultra-conservative parents and friends could not understand what had happened to my husband. Nobody expected him to change so greatly. Occasionally he dropped some vague hints from which followed that he had spoken to *sheikhs*, introduced to him by his friends, who were well-informed about Islam. They explained to him that the majority of Muslims didn't follow the whole Islam; they just chose peaceful and beautiful parts but forgot about violent ones. You have to love your wife but remember to hit her from time to time or she will forget that she is just a woman made for your enjoyment. You ought to treat the infidels well, if it benefits you, but don't forget that your main obligation is to overthrow their government and impose the *Sharia*.

I couldn't believe that my humble hubby was now a faithful Wahabbi. I hoped I was asleep and dreaming, but I was not.

I managed to run away and get to the German embassy. My conversation with a female worker was another eye-opener—she asked me, "When will you learn to listen to the news, stupid hens?" She meant that all women knew that dating a Muslim, let alone marrying one, was a dangerous affair, yet we didn't pay attention to all the warnings. Why do we keep on dating them?

Luckily, my children are with me, thanks to good lawyers. I am working and enjoying my life. But it could have been different. In that case, I could only blame myself for my stupidity.

CHAPTER TWENTY-TWO

"REAL" ISLAM

"Islam today is the most hated religion in the world. The words 'Islam' and 'fundamentalism' are associated with terrorism, genocide, murder, bombing, hate—anything that goes against humanity. This has caused a great deal of pain, anxiety, panic and insecurity amongst the Islamists."

ABUL KASEM, a real person who lives and breathes Australian air, writes his testimony from the great city of Sydney where he has vowed not to cave in to fear and to speak the truth about the effects of Islam on his native Bangladesh, a country he once called home and still loves.

Abul's letter describes witnessing the genocide of Bengalis at the hands of an Islamic army. As a result, he has devoted his life to opposing the spread of Islam. The question aɪɪses: If this is what an Islamic army did to Bengalis, what would they do to Americans?

Abul's Testimony

My name is Abul Kasem. I am a native of Bangladesh, a Muslim majority country. Currently, I am an Australian. During my childhood and adulthood, which I spent in the Islamic society of Bangladesh, I witnessed how Islam has decidedly rendered our rich Bengali culture to the servitude of Arab Bedouin culture. Islam has robbed the very essence of our Bengalihood. In 1971, in the genocide of Bengalis by the Islamic army of Pakistan, I experienced the true color of Islam—it was inhumane, barbaric, and imperialistic. My personal experience forced me to ponder deeply what I always believed to be infallible words of Allah in the Qur'an, and the personal actions of his messenger Mohammad. I took Islam very seriously, spent many years reading and comprehending the "real Islam," just to satisfy myself that I was not wrong in my understanding of Islam.

The result is that I had no choice but to leave this terrible cult of hate, terror, destruction, and savagery. Islam is the opposite of civilization. In these few passages you will learn more about my perception of Islam.

An Islamist is like an addict of a hardcore drug. The more you tell him about the truth of the drug "Islam," the more he will cling to it. In fact, he cannot live without the drug. But deep inside he knows for sure that he is under the influence of a powerful drug and what is going on around today's world is truly inspired by the doctrine of "true or real Islam."

It is like smoking. Most smokers know the potential danger of smoking yet they cling to it despite so much warning by the government and the medical doctors.

However, we should not get disappointed with this. I myself was one of these drug addicts. I used to think in exactly the same way that these Islamists are reacting whenever they see the truth. It is not that simple for these people to give up their faith. In fact, we should never even say that they should do this. Because this will surely be counterproductive. All we do is just show them the picture. Let them go and deny. But they are definitely agitated; if not they would not even bother to respond. The agitation of their mind and their denial is the clearest signal that the message has gone through although there is denial. This is what we do; that is, we create some doubt and a little confusion. It will take some time before the next stage sets in. In this stage they may even turn more to their religion. This is another sign that a Muslim is desperate to make sure that what he believes is correct. This may continue for some time.

At some point during this stage he may suddenly wake up and have a second look at his irrational belief. This is the time he will slowly stop practicing his rituals and read more about what we write. This is the time when we win.

I receive plenty of hate mail and even threats to my life. Almost all of them call me a traitor. All this hate mail proves is that my message is causing agitation and the Islamists are feeling insecure. Whenever I receive hate mail I become quite confident that the message has hit the target. I do not bother even to respond to these hate messages. Time will take care of everything. We just plant the seed of doubt, that's all. Leave the rest to nature. It will take care of itself.

Let me also tell you that I have received quite a few sincere e-mails from Muslims who told me that they have left Islam after carefully examining the pros and cons. No Muslim will announce publicly that he has left Islam; therefore, be certain that most Muslims will seldom tell you that they have left Islam.

Therefore, we should not at all get disappointed when we receive irrational/hate mail from the Islamists. It will take a very long time (probably a century) before we can see any visible and tangible result of our effort. I will have died by that time. To me, that is fine. I do not expect a billion Muslims to discard their religion overnight simply by reading a few articles. This is not going to happen. The path to enlightenment is extremely slow.

Please kindly note that without the advent of the Internet we could not have even gotten what we have achieved today. The Internet has changed everything. You can see that so many Web sites are now telling the truth about the "real Islam." Even a few years ago these were unthinkable for the Muslims. I myself got most of the truth about Islam from the Internet.

Therefore, we need some patience. Islam today is the most hated religion in the world. The words "Islam" and "fundamentalism" are associated with terrorism, genocide, murder, bombing, hate—anything that goes against humanity. This has caused a great deal of pain, anxiety, panic, and insecurity amongst the Islamists. They know rather well that it is the Internet and the extraordinary power of the electronic media that is their enemy. That is why the Islamists are scanning the entire cyber world to monitor what the world is thinking about Islam and they are determined to counter the truth with falsehood and deception even if they have to twist their own holy scriptures for this.

I have tried to give you my idea on how to respond to an Islamist. The best response is no active response. We just portray the "real Islam" and let the Islamists think.

CHAPTER TWENTY-THREE

LIVING WITNESSES VS. POLITICAL CORRECTNESS

"What if—despite our deepest hopes and wishes—Islam is not, at its core, a basically good, peaceful, and tolerant religion? What if Islam at its core is actually very similar to Nazism or any number of other misguided or even evil belief systems, and does in fact want to dominate the world?"

HAVING CONCLUDED the testimony portion of the book, one resounding element seems to stand out. Despite the endless claims of Muslim apologists, when Islam displays outstanding measures of personal freedoms or tolerance of non-Muslims, it is the exception and not the norm. As we all know by now, the goal of radical Islam is to bring about complete Islamic global domination.

If the Islamists are not stopped, then what you have read here—the stories of oppression, intolerance, and the extreme discrimination that the West left behind decades ago—will eventually be told, not from the other side of the world, but from our own neighborhoods. If the Islamists are not stopped, then the accounts of those you have read here could become part of the daily lives of future generations in the West. If you think this is a preposterous notion then consider the following: Whether or not we choose to ignore the facts, the Islamic world and the West are currently involved in a holy war. And the West does not appear to be winning. In truth, there are people who are prepared to die and kill us simply because we do not embrace Islam as they do. Additionally, they are also prepared to kill other Muslims, such as Benazair Bhutto, who also do not embrace radical Islam. This reality is further evidenced by the increasing number of news stories citing Allah and Islam as a justification for cold-blooded murder. Indeed, radical Islam's violence and hatred towards Christians, Hindus, Buddhists, and most particularly toward Jews is quite apparent to anyone who reads the newspaper even casually.

As we all know, on September 11, 2001, in addition to the collapse of the Twin Towers, radical Islam also attacked the Pentagon. Yes, in the name of Allah, terrorists targeted the very epicenter of America's military might. This was war executed in the name of Allah. From that moment on, these subsequent years have witnessed waves of evil, all carried out in the name of Islam, and there is no hope of this going away any time soon. In recent years things have most certainly gone from bad to worse.

In truth it is becoming increasingly evident that Islamic fundamentalism is a global problem, and if it is not stopped will soon arrive at a neighborhood near you. By the time that this book goes to print, a host of new stories will no doubt have made the headlines. There are in truth millions of people who want to convert or kill us in the name of Allah. Let us never forget 9/11, 7/11, the Madrid bombings, the Indian train attacks, and the Bali atrocity. Yet, despite the realities of these stories and the testimonies presented in this book since September 11, the West still seems confused regarding the true nature of Islam.

On one hand, we have been told, if once then a thousand times, "Islam means peace" (the truth is that Islam means submission to Allah). We have been told that Islam is a truly beautiful religion and that it is just like any other world religion. We have been assured that Islam is not in any way inherently violent. We have been told that "real Islam" does not support *jihad* or holy war against "infidels." We have been told that those that make up the radical Muslim fringe are only a very tiny minority of the world Muslim population. They have "hijacked a noble religion," we have been told.

Yet among those who have left Islam, we hear a very different account. Are those who talk of the peaceful religion of Islam not in fact talking about the sterilized, decaffeinated, or "Christianized" version of Islam that is specifically packaged for acceptance in the West? Is the diet Islam-lite the real Islam, or is it the Islam that we see on the nightly news? Here's the difficulty: The voices that paint Islam as mild and serene are most often the politicians, or Muslim apologists, or the spokesman for the local mosque.

On the other hand, there is another Islam that we see. This is the Islam that produces far too many violent and even murderous individuals. It is the Islam of Osama bin Laden, Mahmoud Ahmadinejad, and the suicide bombers. It is the Islam of *jihad* and "kill the infidels." This is the Islam that most would simply like to wish away into nonexistence. But now, having read the stories of these brave and dear men and women, the question is now posed: Who will we listen to? Will we continue to accept the claims of the hopeful politicians, the Muslim apologists, and the evangelists funded by the Wahabbi Saudi Arabian government, or will we accept the accounts of those who have actually lived Islam? Will we accept what we are told, or will we accept what we have seen over the past decade on a global scale? Will we ascribe weight to the voices of the scholars who have spent a lifetime studying Islam such as Robert Spencer or Daniel Pipes, or will we believe those who claim that "slaughter the infidels wherever you find them" (*Qur'an 2:191*) really means to "love your neighbor as yourself"?

Whenever any particular story breaks in the news regarding yet another inhuman atrocity that was committed by someone who has come under the influence of Islam, almost reflexively various commentators stumble over themselves to explain and qualify that, despite the acts of a few misguided and underprivileged souls, Islam itself is truly a great and noble religion and is most certainly not to blame. They comfort and reassure us that what we are seeing today with the suicide bombings and the beheadings are simply the actions of a few evil and violent perverts who have "hijacked a great religion."

When we as Westerners make such claims—namely that Islam is at its core a great, peaceful, and good religion—when we make these claims based not on objective realities, such as a solid examination of the various sacred texts and history of Islam, but rather based on our own sheer faith that it simply must be so, we are literally committing cultural suicide. This is not an exaggeration. It is Jonestown on a scale unimaginable. This poison, however, may take a few generations to complete its work, but it is no less effective than the infamous Kool-Aid that was swallowed en-masse in Ghana.

Now, by "faith" we are speaking in two ways. First, we say faith in the sense of a belief system, in this case that vague and yet so popular unnamed belief system that says—and we've all heard the cliché a thousand times—that all religions lead to God and all religions are basically good. We also say faith in the sense of hope—or probably a better word would be desperation. A desperately held belief that Islam simply must be good at its core; otherwise...then what?

It must. It simply must.

But what if it isn't?

Are we allowed to even ask these questions? We can hear the charges of spreading hatred already. Yet, is it truly "hateful" to critique or question an ideology? In other words, isn't hatred directed toward individuals and not concepts or ideologies? Or re-phrased, in the early 1940s, could someone both love the German people and still speak out against Nazism without being accused of hatred? Or another relevant question would be: Is not one of the premier strengths of any truly "progressive" society the ability to freely debate and discuss virtually anything? Is not this one of the greatest strengths of Western culture? Iron sharpens iron. Or is the sound of iron sharpening iron now simply perceived as unnecessary and annoying "negative vibes" that are only to be quieted?

Has the "politically correct" runaway juggernaut of a social experiment already robbed our society of the ability to civilly discuss those things that are oftentimes messy or uncomfortable? Has a hyper-political correctness robbed us of one of the premiere freedoms that truly make us great? In our efforts to become sensitive, have we become absurd? We would argue that we have.

There has also emerged an attempt to explain many of the atrocities that have been carried out in Allah's name. Frequently, the blame is placed on the creation of the state of Israel or American interference in the Middle East—specifically the wars in Afghanistan and Iraq. After all, somewhere deeply ingrained in each of us is the need for a rational explanation as a means through which we can try to solve problems. If we can simply change ourselves, then we could eliminate our enemies' desire to kill us—or so the thinking goes.

Sadly, this belief is based more on fear-based emotionalism, guilt-based self-hatred, and a glaring ignorance of the history of Islam than on any legitimate reasons. It is interesting that back in the 1930s, as Europe faced the looming threat of Nazism, the Roman Catholic historian and intellectual Hilaire Belloc believed that Islam would one day pose an even greater danger than that of Hitler's regime and was acutely aware that historically, "Vienna, as we saw, was almost taken and only saved by the Christian army under the command of the King of Poland on a date that ought to be among the most famous in history—September 11, 1683."[1]

In other words, the Islamic threat existed far before the modern nation of Israel or America existed. In fact, as a few of the former Muslims in this book have cited, the universally accepted sacred traditions of Islam have declared from the very beginning that the day of resurrection cannot come until faithful Muslims carry out a final holocaust against the Jewish people. Is this ancient sacred tradition to be blamed on the state of Israel? At the time of its "inspiration," the Jewish people had no nation to call their own. Yet the anti-Semitic spirit of Islam existed even back then.

This relentless anti-Semitic spirit was perhaps articulated nowhere better than from the lips of Hassan Nasrallah, the leader of the Hezbollah movement in Lebanon, when he said in October of 2002, "If Jews all gather in Israel, it will save us the trouble of going after them worldwide."[2] Is America to blame for this desire to kill all Jews? Or radical Islam's apparent fascination with Adolf Hitler? Indeed, Hitler's *Mein Kempf* has been a bestseller in many Arab nations for more than a decade, especially in Palestine. Given this deep-rooted hatred of Israel and the U.S., is it possible that the attacks on September 11 had nothing to do with our U.S. foreign policy but was simply an attack on America—the largest Christian nation in the world—on the anniversary of the defeat of the Muslim armies by Christendom at the gates of Vienna?

Returning now to the question asked earlier regarding the inherent goodness or evil of Islam. What if—despite our deepest hopes and wishes—Islam is not, at its core, a basically good, peaceful, and tolerant religion? What if Islam at its core is actually very similar to Nazism or any number of other misguided or even evil belief systems and does in fact want to dominate the world? What if Islam has in its foundation many things that are diametrically opposed to freedom of speech, freedom of choice, freedom of expression—or just plain freedom in general? What if the claim that Islam has been hijacked by radicals is not actually true, but instead, the radicals are actually the ones who are most accurately and faithfully following the core tenets of Islam? What if an objective study of Islam showed this to be the case?

As we read through several of these stories, there is a common thread: None were politically correct. Why is this? Why is it that when we try to discern and discuss the true nature of Islam, that we are quick to listen to those who only discuss Islam in positive or glowing terms, but we refuse to believe the conclusions of those scholars who have spent a lifetime studying Islam and who have concluded just the opposite? Or more importantly, why would we be quick to reject the real and very personal stories of the actual people who were both born and raised in Islam? Why is it that the picture that is painted in the many stories told in this book is not one that is even considered by many in the media or the educational system? Why until now have we chosen to put political correctness above mere reality? And now, having heard the warnings presented here, will we choose to continue to bow in mindless devotion to the altar of political correctness or will we choose to heed the warnings of these courageous living witnesses?

AFTERWORD

WHERE TO FROM HERE?
BY GREGORY M. DAVIS

THOSE WHO HAVE SEEN ISLAM from the inside know better than anyone its true colors. It is their testimonies—more than the politically correct sophistry of contemporary Western commentators—that we must heed if we are to survive the resurgence of Islam on the world stage. The mounting news accounts of apparently unrelated acts of violence, "unrest," and terrorism from around the world alarm many, but few possess the patience or clarity of thought to bring such apparently disparate events into focus. In fact, the overwhelming preponderance of organized violence on the world stage today—from Nigeria to Thailand, from Bosnia to Bali, from Chechnya to the Philippines, from Sudan to Indonesia, from Israel to Kashmir, to Paris, London, Madrid, Moscow, Washington, and New York—has its roots in the simple faith of Mohammad.

Across the globe, now as in Islam's heyday (from roughly the Muslim invasions of the Holy Land and Spain in the seventh and eighth centuries A.D. to the Turks' near-capture of Vienna at the end of the seventeenth), Islamic *jihad* is making itself felt. While there is no "central command" that orchestrates the global *jihad*, there is a common playbook: the Qur'an and the life and example of Mohammad, the *Sunnah*. If the West continues to misunderstand this basic fact, there can be little hope that it will take the necessary measures of self-defense. We are not threatened merely by the occasional terrorist but by a cohesive ideology, which for a thousand years threatened to overwhelm the West and managed to overcome other civilizations manifestly more advanced than itself. Ask the Persians or the Byzantines.

Much today is written and verbalized about terrorism, but little about Islam itself. We must understand that terrorism as such is not the enemy. Islam is not terrorism and terrorism is not Islam. Terrorism is a tactic to destabilize a political order and, ultimately, replace it with something else. There is no substitute to discerning the ultimate objectives of one's adversary. It is the goal of Islamic terrorism that we must come to understand if we are to counter it. Like the casual use of "religion," the flinging about of "terrorism" serves to obscure the specifically Islamic nature of the problem. The *jihadis'* goal is not a united Ireland or an end to animal testing but the realization of the global order of Allah, *Sharia* law, as dictated by their holy book and the example of their Prophet. We must be willing to get our hands dirty in the sources of Islamic inspiration—the Qur'an and the *Sunnah*—if we are to respond effectively to Islam's war against us.

The reasons that an individual Muslim will one day awaken to the call of *jihad* are surely as varied as individuals themselves. In any ideological community, there will always be a subset of true believers willing to sacrifice themselves for their beliefs. This subset moves and draws strength from immersion in a sympathetic milieu of other, perhaps less orthodox, faithful. The great mass of believers need not practice, or even subscribe to, the full tenets of their faith to afford a space in which true believers can and will. And it is these true believers who serve as the community's vanguard in its efforts to realize its ultimate goals. Why are there so few "moderate" Muslim voices? Precisely because they would necessarily clash with the voices of their orthodox co-religionists who, in any Islamic context, must get the better part of the argument. While there may have been many "moderate" Mensheviks in the early Communist movement, it was inevitable, in light of the very assumptions of Communist ideology, that the more ruthless Bolsheviks would gain the upper hand. The upshot is that, as the general Muslim population in the West continues to grow—and its growth is only being encouraged by the Western secular powers—so will its nuclei of true-believing *jihadis*.

It is important to realize that the subversion of Western secular government by the *Sharia* agenda may be furthered through means other than terrorism. In the West, Muslim activists are increasingly availing themselves of other, legal forms of subversion and intimidation. Those for whom the ends justify the means can readily force an open society, which extends the benefit of the doubt as a matter of course, back on its heels. One of the ongoing debates in Muslim communities, both in the Islamic world and in the West, is whether a more Fabian strategy would serve the long-term *jihad* better than the bin Laden approach. Already, substantial parts of major European cities—Paris, London, Rotterdam, Malmo—are effectively ruled by *Sharia* law, enforced by local imams and their true-believing followers. And while Islam continues to grow in leaps and bounds, the native European populations are collapsing, a trend that has been underway for decades. Never in the history of the world has a materially sated civilization simply refused to reproduce. It seems that Europe, having jettisoned its Christian spirituality in order to glory the more in this life, is finding it difficult even to stay alive.

But to those ensconced in the halls of power, it is unimaginable that the edifice of modern civilization could be seriously threatened by an ancient religion from the wastelands of Arabia—an attitude one might have found in Cairo, Antioch, Persia, Spain, Constantinople, and countless other places before they were overrun by Mohammad's "primitive" followers. We must bear in mind that, for most of the past thirteen centuries, Europe and Christendom had to battle for their lives against Islamic imperialism. At times, it was a close-run thing. However permanent it may seem, the relative quiet we have enjoyed on the Islam front since the Roman Catholic victory at Vienna on September 11, 1683—a day on the calendar to be remembered forever for a victory of a very different sort—is more the exception than the rule. We are not today facing Arab or Ottoman armies massing at the gates; rather we are witnessing the transformation from within of Western centers of strength into Islamic centers of power, permitted by a ruling class if not actually collaborationist then at least criminally incompetent. Political struggles invariably subtend factors of both capacity and will; while weaker in the former, Islam's growing confidence—its *faith*—more than makes up for it in the latter.

While, on the one hand, Islam possesses the dynamism and staying power of a major religious faith, it shares the political objectives of modern totalitarian projects such as Communism and National Socialism—an exceptionally dangerous combination. Like Communism and National Socialism, Islam seeks the conquest and submission of territory to a particular political and legal regime, in its case, *Sharia* law. Like Communism and National Socialism, Islam divides the world into two warring spheres, one intrinsically good, the other evil. *Dar al-Islam*, the House of Islam, is the territory enlightened by *Sharia* law; *dar al-harb*, the House of War, the rest of the world upon which war is to be made until it is brought permanently into the *Sharia* fold. It is one of the great ironies of our time that tremendous political energy is expended on keeping Western public life thoroughly sanitized of the West's traditional religion, Christianity, while Islam, an ideology that *explicitly* conflates—or rather never distinguishes in the first place—between the political and the religious, is blithely allowed in through the front door.

Despite its political nature, Islam continues to shelter under the rubric "religion," a vague, sentimental term used to forestall rigorous inquiry into the thing itself. Among elite circles today, "religion" connotes quaint mythologies and rituals of more primitive, and therefore morally unimpeachable, peoples. (The exception, of course, is Christianity, the white man's perennial instrument of tyranny.) The "orientalism" decried by that scourge of honest scholarship, Edward Said, is more alive today in the minds of his intellectual progeny than anywhere in the more serious Western scholarship of days gone by.

One of the difficulties for Westerners in coming to grips with the Islamic danger is that, since the French Revolution, the dangers that have threatened the West on a civilizational scale have arisen from within its own intellectual traditions. Communism and National Socialism, for example, were tumorous growths that perverted aspects of Western thought to catastrophic lengths. Such "-isms" of modernity are rightly characterized as "extreme," having distorted the West's own traditions of communal and national ideals. But such labels have little meaning in the context of Islam, an ideology with a decidedly non-Western pedigree. In the struggles against Communism and National Socialism, the healthful part of the Western organism managed to beat back the disease, and has since built up immunity to such forms of political cancer. But like the effects of chemotherapy, the treatment, while fighting the malignance, has enfeebled the body. The hypersensitivity in the West today—especially in Western Europe—to anything invocative of national pride or civilizational identity has crippled its ability to assert the legitimacy of its own traditions against those who would destroy them. The danger today comes not from some new perversion of the Western tradition but from an alien ideology whose lineage stems not from Athens and Jerusalem but Mecca and Medina. As usual, many are still fighting the last war.

But the most salient manifestations of the Islamic tradition today, the terrorist and the suicide bomber, are no "extreme" distortions of a benign Islamic tradition; rather they are manifestations of that tradition itself. The "-ism" that political correctitude requires appended to "Islam" and "*jihad*" whenever there is mention of Muslims and violence is both entirely redundant and fundamentally misleading. Unlike the case of true Western radicals, there is no hope of recapturing Islam's true believers back into the Western fold; there is no error to be corrected that will set them back on their true, benign path. The gravest mistake of the West today is its insistent hope in a fictive "moderate" Islam.

The persistent myth of a peaceful Islam, which lacks any doctrinal or historical basis, serves to forestall any decisive remedial action and, if not soon relinquished, will doom both the West and those individual Muslims susceptible to transformation. The only "peace" afforded with respect to Islam derives from a calculation of force: either overwhelming superior force, which keeps Islamic predations contained, or abject surrender, which slates the *jihad*. The prime fault of the progressive Western mind is ever to look toward what might be rather than to accept what is. Islam is what it is: a violent, expansionary political program with aspirations of world conquest. If it ever transforms into something else, it will not be by virtue of infidel hopes and blandishments, however earnest.

The West's continuing self-deception that its liberal political ways may be squared with Islam is the basis for its ongoing policy mistakes, both foreign and domestic. In the belief that Iraq could be transformed into a Western-style "democracy," America has expended significant blood and fantastic treasure on replacing a largely secular dictator (and former ally) with an Islamic theocracy. Similarly, the Western European powers are setting themselves up for a severe disappointment in trying to mold what is now tragicomically referred to as the "Euro-Mediterraean Union," i.e., Eurabia. Indeed, the growth of Islam in Europe is rapidly confronting the European populations with a choice of catastrophes: (a) continue to treat Islam as a "lifestyle choice" and quietly slip behind the iron veil of *Sharia* sometime in the latter half of the century; (b) summarily abandon the modern assumptions on which the welfare state and its suicidal concomitants, multiculturalism and revolutionary levels of immigration, are based; (c) manage the rising tide of European Islam and *jihadi* terrorism through the construction of a police state. In light of European history of the past few centuries, the importation of Islam into Europe precisely to serve as a pretext for constructing an Orwellian society cannot be ruled out. Indeed, such a hypothesis explains quite neatly why it is that the European elite would so willingly sign the death warrant of their own civilization. It may be that the mousey Eurocrats are quietly effecting what the Communist and fascist revolutionaries failed to accomplish on a permanent basis—a pan-European police state. The only other alternative, (d), increasingly likely, is what we have seen so many times before, in Lebanon, in Bosnia, in Kosovo: civil war. While it may be hard to imagine urban warfare in London and Paris, it was hard to imagine in Sarajevo and Beirut, too.

If a serious defense of Western civilization is to take place, it must first begin with a frank acknowledgement of the political nature of Islam. It is imperative to reclassify Islam as a political system with religious aspects rather than as a religion with political aspects. Islam is in fact an alternative form of government in competition with Western governments that seeks to weaken and, ultimately, destroy and replace them. It is both false and perilous for Western societies to regard Islam as a "religion" and afford it the special protection associated with that term. Under the guise of "religious freedom," Muslim activists will continue to subvert Western governments first politically and then by force. Such has become commonplace in Western Europe in which acts of violence are used to intimidate and cow populations in order to prepare the way for political demands.

Islam must not be afforded the protected status of a religion precisely because it does not recognize the separation of religion and politics on which Western-style government and religious freedom are based. Any recognition of legitimacy must be reciprocal: It is illogical—and suicidal—for Western governments to regard Islam as a legitimate "religion" when Islam is unwilling to recognize the legitimacy of those same governments.

The West must awaken to the fact that it is facing nothing less than the resurgence of the greatest war machine in world history: an ideology that holds the killing of others, the plundering of their wealth, the conquering of their lands, the enslavement of their people, and the destruction of their institutions to be among the highest virtues and the stepping stones to salvation. The only appropriate policy will be one of containing Islam: keeping it out of our own societies while being very realistic about our ability to influence affairs in its sphere of influence. First and foremost, we must abandon the fantasy that asymptotic globalization will somehow prove the cure to Islam's fourteen-hundred-yearold antipathy to the rest of the world. Those reluctant to accept the bleak truth should ask themselves: Is their reluctance the result of careful study of the Islamic sources and history, or is it due to their unwillingness to accept a grim reality that will necessitate sacrifice and struggle? Almost invariably it seems, Islam's non-Muslim apologists lack even a basic understanding of the subject they so imperiously pronounce on. For those who know better, we must not hesitate to take such people to task, to expose their ignorance, their dishonesty, and their intellectual laziness.

It is a paradox, but no society that has survival as its highest goal will survive: It must possess a higher, transcendent end to motivate its people to defend the social order against potential attack. Belief in a higher reality that transcends this world reassures the warrior, whether his art is scholarly or martial, that fighting—and, if necessary, dying—is worth it. Facing a spiritually denuded West, this is Islam's great strength. Today, everything that once made the West great and that distinguished it from other civilizations—overseas expansion, Christianity, superior cultural achievement—has been delegitimated by decades of relativist battering. Recovering the great cultural inheritance of Western civilization—so carelessly squandered by its supposed guardians—will be the great requisite to Western survival.

It is evident that Islam has its true believers—do we have ours?

Gregory M. Davis, Ph.D.
Author of *Religion of Peace? Islam's War Against the World*
Producer and director of *Islam: What the West Needs to Know*

CONTRIBUTORS

Editor Susan Crimp is the author of eight books, including a biography of Rose Kennedy which she co-authored with Cindy Adams. Crimp authored *Touched by a Saint*, a biography of Mother Teresa. She has also worked as a journalist and television producer in America as well as contributing to Britain's *Hello* magazine. Susan recently co- produced *Blues By the Beach*, a documentary which investigated a suicide bombing in Tel Aviv and which won first place at the Hampton's Film Festival in 2005; it also took the Pierre Salinger award at the Avilgon Film Festival in New York in 2006.

Editor Joel Richardson (pseudonym) is an independent religious scholar who has lived and worked in the Middle East. He has been deeply involved in Christian-Muslim interfaith dialogue and is an expert in Christian and Muslim apocalyptic traditions. The author of *Anti-Christ: Islam's Awaited Messiah*, Joel uses a pseudonym in all published works because of threats against his life and the life of his family due to public and private dialogues with Muslims who wished to leave Islam.

Contributors Many of the essays and letters collected in this volume are written by individuals of no great renown. They speak from a rare position within Islam, and are considered apostates and heretics by their own families and friends. Yet they speak bravely of what they have experienced. Some will reveal their identities as the book is close to publication, while others will remain, for the sake of their own safety or that of their families remaining in Muslim countries or neighborhoods, necessarily anonymous. Their credentials are won not in previous publications or in fought-for fame, but in the honesty and integrity of their own stories, told from within a system of bro-kenness and violence.

The compilers, deeply involved in interfaith dialogue for many years, collected these testimonies from individuals met through various social and religious networks which provide safe places of conversation and growth for ex-Muslims. More than one hundred testimonies were collected, and the twenty included here represent the widest variety of voice and experience of those.

Other contributors have received much attention for their writings and statements on radical Islam including:

Dr. Parvin Darabi is an Iranian-born American activist and writer who studied at California State University Northridge, University of Southern California, Pepperdine University, and California Coast University. Parvin worked as an electronic systems engineer, program manager, company president, and engineering consultant until 1994. From 1985-1990, she owned and operated her own company, PT Enterprises in Mountain View, California, where they developed the most sensitive radar detector presently on the German naval vessels active in NATO. Her elder sister, Homa Da-rabi, committed suicide in 1994 by burning herself in a public square in Iran to protest against the Iranian government. Since then, Parvin has become an activist, writing the book *Rage Against the Veil* and speaking out on many occasions against Iran's gov-ernment and the religion of Islam as whole.

Walid Shoebat is an American citizen, born in Palestine, and a former terrorist. As a member of the Palestine Liberation Organi-zation, he took part in terrorist attacks against Israeli targets. Since leaving radical Islam and the life of a terrorist, he has founded the Walid Shoebat Foundation, an organization that seeks to combat anti-Semitism and promote peace in the Middle East. Shoebat has appeared numerous times on national media outlets such as CNN, MSNBC, CBS, and BBC. He is the author of several books, and a sought-after speaker across the globe.

Gregory M. Davis studied political religions and totalitarianism at Stanford University, where he received his Ph.D. in political science in 2003. He has written for *Human Events, WorldNetDaily,* and *FrontPage Magazine,* has been a regular contributor to Jihad Watch, and has appeared as a guest commentator on Fox News and numerous radio programs across America. He is author of *Religion of Peace? Islam's War Against the World* and producer and director of the feature documentary *Islam: What the West Needs to Know.*

NOTES

1. Matt Cherry and Warren Allen Smith, "One Brave Woman vs. Religious Fundamentalism: An Interview with Taslima Nasrin," *Free Inquiry*, Volume 19: Number 1, winter 1998-1999, http://www.secularhumanism.org/index.php?section=library&page=nasrin_19_1.

2. Islamic Republic News Agency, "President: Rule of Islam only way for salvation of mankind," August 14, 2007, http://www2.irna.ir/en/news/view/menu-234/ 0708142013173859.htm.

3. Raymond Ibrahim, "200 Million Minority: Islam's apologists completely miss the point," *National Review Online*, May 8, 2007, http://article.nationalreview.com/?q=MWRlNjJmNzU4NzZkZDk 0NDgxNDMzMWEwMmNhMzJmYzE=.

4. Khaled Waleed, "The Real Face of Islam," in *Why We Left Islam: Former Muslims Speak Out*, ed. Susan Crimp and Joel Richardson, 11-14 (Los Angeles, CA: WND Books, 2008).

Introduction

1. BBC News, "'Mohammad' teddy bear teacher arrested," Nov. 26, 2007, http://news.bbc.co.uk/2/hi/africa/7112929.stm.

2. BBC News, "Mohammad cartoon row intensifies," February 1, 2006, http://news.bbc.co.uk/2/hi/europe/4670370.stm.

3. BBC News, "Italian nun shot dead in Somalia," September 18, 2006, http://news.bbc.co.uk/2/hi/africa/5353850.stm.

4. BBC News, "Letter fails to improve US-Iran ties," May 9, 2006, http://news.bbc.co.uk/2/hi/middle_east/4754161.stm.

5. BBC News, Benazir Bhutto killed in attack," December 27, 2007, http://news.bbc.co.uk/2/hi/south_asia/7161590.stm.

6. *Sahih Bukhari*, Volume 9, Book 84, Number 57.

7. George, Bruce, *Harbottle's Dictionary of Battles* (Granada, London: Van Nostrand Reinhold, 1979).

8. Martin Mawyer, "Sheikh Mubarak Gilani Forms Terrorist Compounds Inside United States," Christian Action Network, http://www.christianaction.org/Special_Projects/Sheikh_Gilani_Ln.htm.

9. Ibid.

10. Ibid.

11. Ibid.

12. Ibid.

13. Ibid.

14. Paul L. Williams, Ph.D., "Radical Muslim paramilitary compound flourishes in upper New York state," Canada Free Press, May 11, 2007, http://www.canadafreepress.com/2007/paul-williams051107.htm.

15. Ibid.

16. Ibid.

17. Ibid.

18. Bernard Lewis, "Islam and Liberal Democracy," *Atlantic Monthly*, February, 1993.

Chapter One: My Sister

1. Parvin Darabi and Romin P. Thomson, *Rage Against the Veil* (Amherst, NY: Prometheus Books, 1999), 17.

2. *Sahih Bukhari*, Volume 4, Book 54, Number 464. Found in the University of Southern California-Muslim Student Association Compendium of Islamic Texts.

3. *Qur'an*, trans. M. H. Shakir, 10th ed. (Elmhurst, NY: Tahrike Tarsile, 1999), back cover.

4. Sheikh Abdur Rahman Abdul Kaliq, "The Wisdom Behind the Islamic Laws Regarding Women," prepared for the United Nations Fourth World Conference on Women, Beijing, China, January 15, 1995 (Ann Arbor, MI: Islamic Assembly of North America), page 17.

5. Ayatollah Khomeini, *The Little Green Book: Sayings of Ayatollah Khomeini*, trans. Harold Salemson (New York, NY: Bantam Books, 1979), I:6.

6. Ibid., II:19.

7. This law is based on Qur'an 2:28; see also al-Tabari, 4:27; al-Razi, 9:203.

8. Cited in Parvin Darabi, "Establishment of the Islamic Republic in Iran & The Present Situation for Women," Dr. Homa Darabi Foundation Web site, http://www.homa.org/Details.asp? ContentID=2137352848&TOCID=2

Chapter Three: Redemption

1. Council on Foreign Relations, "A Nonpartisan Resource for Information and Analysis Entry: Jamaat al-Islamiyya, Egyptian Islamic Jihad," updated October 2005, http://www.cfr.org/publication/9156/.

Chapter Seven: I Am an Ex-Muslim and Proud of It!

1. Anthony Browne, "Muslim apostates cast out and at risk from faith and family," *London Times*, February 5, 2005.

Chapter Twenty-Three: Living Witnesses Versus Political Correctness.

1. Hilaire Belloc, *The Great Heresies* (Rockford, NY: Tan Books and Publishers, 1991), 70-71.

2. Quoted in Michael Rubin, "Eradication first before diplomacy," *National Review*, July 17, 2006, http://article.nationalreview.com/?q=MDZmY2E1YjY3YTRlOGYwN2IzNGEzODU2ZDNiMmJiM2I=.

Read these other Titles from WND!